"*Leveraging AI for Human-Centered Learning* offers educators a thoughtful roadmap for navigating the rise of artificial intelligence in the classroom without losing sight of what makes learning profoundly human. As schools embrace AI's potential, this book ensures that students' social-emotional growth and cultural identities remain at the heart of teaching. Through practical strategies and critical insights, Dr. Marlee S. Bunch and Brittany R. Collins empower educators to leverage AI tools in ways that deepen connection, foster equity, and uphold the essential human elements of education in an ever-evolving digital landscape."
—**Errol St. Clair Smith,** Executive Producer of BAM Education Radio Network

"What makes teachers so important is their adaptability. Through pandemics, new approaches, and a changing political landscape that warp classroom teaching (past and present), teachers have stuck it out. The teachers I have gotten to know at this stage in my life, as a high school senior, have shaped me in a multitude of ways. They've shown me the role of empathy, hard work, stick-to-itiveness, irony, disillusionment, and honesty in learning inside and outside of the classroom. I or anyone else can't surely determine what direction academia will go in with regard to AI, but I do know that as long as teachers such as Dr. Bunch and Ms. Collins, among many others, are as focused and passionate as before, students are in good hands. At least as long as evil robots don't attack."
—**Cameron Alleyne,** student, from the Afterword

Leveraging AI for Human-Centered Learning

Leveraging AI for Human-Centered Learning provides intentional approaches to the integration of artificial intelligence tools into middle and high school classrooms, specifically to foster equity and social-emotional well-being. The overlap of AI with today's schools poses pivotal questions about ethics, morality, inclusion, and human learning at a time when students are already reckoning with public health crises, systemic injustice, and other connected challenges. This book helps teachers examine the pros and cons of artificial intelligence—as used by both educators and students—as well as its implications for meaningful culturally responsive teaching and social-emotional learning efforts. Featuring activities, lesson plans, and discussion and writing prompts for use with adolescent learners, each chapter offers concrete pedagogical approaches and instructional innovations that align technological changes with learning objectives in ways that advance, rather than replace or neutralize, attention to equity and well-being.

Marlee S. Bunch is an interdisciplinary educator, author, and scholar. Her research examines the oral histories of Black female educators in Hattiesburg, Mississippi who taught between 1954 and 1970. She is the founder of the un/HUSH teaching framework and author of *The Magnitude of Us* and *Unlearning the Hush*.

Brittany R. Collins is the Director of Education at Write the World, Inc., a nonprofit dedicated to closing opportunity gaps in writing education. She also works as an educational consultant and professional development facilitator focused on trauma-informed teaching, social-emotional learning, and literacy education.

Also Available from Routledge
Eye On Education
(www.routledge.com/k-12)

Making Technology Work in Schools, 2nd edition:
How PK-12 Educators Can Foster Digital-Age Learning
By Timothy D. Green, Loretta C. Donovan,
Jody Peerless Green

Artificial Intelligence in Schools:
A Guide for Teachers, Administrators,
and Technology Leaders
By Varun Arora

Teaching as Protest:
Emancipating Classrooms Through Racial Consciousness
By Robert Harvey, Susan Gonzowitz

Abolitionist Leadership in Schools:
Undoing Systemic Injustice Through Communally
Conscious Education
By Robert Harvey

Leading Schools Through Trauma:
A Data-Driven Approach to Helping Children Heal
By Michael S. Gaskell

Leveraging AI for Human-Centered Learning

Culturally Responsive and Social-Emotional Classroom Practice in Grades 6–12

Marlee S. Bunch and Brittany R. Collins

NEW YORK AND LONDON

First published 2025
by Routledge
605 Third Avenue, New York, NY 10158

and by Routledge
4 Park Square, Milton Park, Abingdon, Oxon, OX14 4RN

Routledge is an imprint of the Taylor & Francis Group, an informa business

© 2025 Marlee S. Bunch and Brittany R. Collins

The right of Marlee S. Bunch and Brittany R. Collins to be identified as authors of this work has been asserted in accordance with sections 77 and 78 of the Copyright, Designs and Patents Act 1988.

All rights reserved. No part of this book may be reprinted or reproduced or utilized in any form or by any electronic, mechanical, or other means, now known or hereafter invented, including photocopying and recording, or in any information storage or retrieval system, without permission in writing from the publishers.

Trademark notice: Product or corporate names may be trademarks or registered trademarks, and are used only for identification and explanation without intent to infringe.

ISBN: 978-1-032-83967-7 (hbk)
ISBN: 978-1-032-80499-6 (pbk)
ISBN: 978-1-003-51029-1 (ebk)

DOI: 10.4324/9781003510291

Typeset in Palatino
by Apex CoVantage, LLC

> This is a jar of us and it gives.
> Other things are meant to float by.
> It's an ocean over there.
> Hear it. Here we are standing.
> You have always been with me.
> That's just how my heart works. . .
>
> —Emily Pettit

We dedicate this text to our friends, students, mentors, and family members—both biological and chosen—on whose shoulders we stand, who have given to us their inspiration and empowered us to dream and become.

And to those no longer here, but with us always in memory, their legacies living on through our work.

Contents

Foreword xi
Fay Cobb Payton
Meet the Authors xv
Acknowledgments xvii

Introduction 1
Marlee S. Bunch

Poetic Reflection: Grounded Generation 17
Jordan Stempleman

1 **What Is AI, Anyway? An Overview for Educators** 19
Brittany R. Collins

Poetic Reflection: Hang Onto It 37
Jordan Stempleman

2 **Applying AI to Human-Centered Pedagogy
Part I: Culturally Responsive Teaching** 39
Marlee S. Bunch

Poetic Reflection: Beside the Vending Machine 77
Jordan Stempleman

3 **Applying AI to Human-Centered Pedagogy Part II:
Social-Emotional Learning** 79
Brittany R. Collins

Poetic Reflection: How to Begin 110
Jordan Stempleman

4 **Using AI to Integrate Cultural Responsiveness and SEL Into English Language Arts** 111
Brittany R. Collins

Poetic Reflection: Wait Here 146
Jordan Stempleman

5 **Enhancing Equitable History Instruction Through AI** 151
Marlee S. Bunch

Epilogue: Looking Ahead 161
Marlee S. Bunch and Brittany R. Collins

Poetic Reflection: Gray Replaces White 165
Jordan Stempleman

Appendices 167
Marlee S. Bunch and Brittany R. Collins

Afterword 185
Cameron Alleyne

Foreword

Fay Cobb Payton

Dr. Fay Cobb Payton, PhD, MBA, is Special Advisor to the Chancellor on Inclusive Innovation; Director of the Institute for Data, Research, and Innovation Science; Professor of Mathematics and Computer Science; and Affiliate Faculty in the Rutgers New Jersey Medical School at Rutgers University–Newark. Visit her website at http://cobbpayton.com.

Artificial intelligence (AI) is increasingly becoming an integral tool in educational settings, offering both opportunities and challenges. AI can personalize learning experiences, automate administrative tasks, provide tutoring support, and enhance accessibility for students with diverse needs. Algorithms can analyze student data, identify learning patterns, and provide targeted interventions to support student progress—all of which offer the promises of technological advances. Dr. Marlee S. Bunch and Brittany R. Collins highlight the uses of AI tools like ChatGPT and MagicSchool to generate everything from lesson plans to Universal Design for Learning concepts.

While the authors clearly delineate the promises of AI, the book also captures the need to incorporate culturally inclusive frameworks to better ensure equity in teaching and learning processes. With this, there are important considerations to not only think about but act on. AI should be designed to recognize and respond to cultural differences in learning styles, communication, and knowledge systems. Ensuring equitable access to AI tools and addressing potential biases in AI systems are crucial concerns. Education systems cannot be decoupled from broadband and digital access.

Several obstacles need to be addressed to ensure AI promotes inclusivity in education. The lack of inclusive representation in AI development and evaluation is a cause for concern. There is a need for clear data governance and protection practices at all levels of the education system. Ethical considerations, including privacy issues and the potential perpetuation of biases, must be carefully examined. Educators and policymakers should focus on developing AI literacy among students, parents, and teachers. After all, AI is not going away, has historically been with and among us, and is embedded in the lived experience. There is a need to explore and act on how AI can incorporate Indigenous ways of knowing and language differences and support diverse cultural perspectives in education.

As we move forward, the content in this book offers the opportunity to embrace and think interdisciplinarily about the content provided in teaching and learning. In doing so, students gain computational skills and become better problem-solvers in an AI world. Rather than avoid or ban AI tools in the classroom, rich interactions, discussions, and problem-solving can lend themselves to address societal and community needs. These interactions can offer teachers and educators the opportunities to include issues of ethical and responsible AI uses in the classroom. Asking and inspiring students to think critically about AI (or any technology along with its impacts) can bolster new ideas and encourage them to evaluate information sources and reliability to identify what is "mis(dis)information" (Cobb Payton, 2024, p. 1), recognize AI applications in daily life, and connect concepts across disciplines, such as computer science, mathematics, ethics, social studies, language arts, and the arts.

By addressing these considerations, we can ensure that AI has the potential to enhance culturally responsive teaching practices and create more inclusive learning environments. We must, however, remember and act accordingly: AI is not and should not be the decider of our children's education. It only provides recommendations. How AI is used alongside humans must be at the forefront, even and especially in education, where inequity continues to be an inescapable challenge.

To explore these and other issues, I invite you to dive into the following pages as Marlee and Brittany show you how to maintain human-centered aspects of teaching while also incorporating AI in a culturally responsive manner.

Reference

Cobb Payton, F. (2024, August 1). When the algorithm hallucinates: Disinformation-misinformation results. *Forbes*. www.forbes.com/sites/faycobbpayton/2024/07/29/when-the-algorithm-hallucinates-disinformation-misinformation-results/

Meet the Authors

Dr. Marlee S. Bunch & Brittany R. Collins

Dr. Marlee S. Bunch, EdD, MEd, MS, BA is an interdisciplinary educator, author, and scholar. Her research examines the oral histories of Black female educators in Hattiesburg, Mississippi who taught between 1954 and 1970. She is the author of *The Magnitude of Us: An Educator's Guide to Creating Culturally Responsive Classrooms* (Teachers College Press, 2024) and *Unlearning the Hush: Oral Histories of Black Female Educators in Mississippi in the Civil Rights Era* (University of Illinois Press, 2025). She has created educational programming for educators and students through the University of Illinois, Rockhurst University, Race Project Kansas City, Smith College, and the Illinois State Board of Education, among others.

She received her doctoral degree from the University of Illinois in education/policy/organizational leadership. Additionally, she has a master's in education (MEd), a master's in gifted education (MS), a bachelor's in English, a certification in gifted education, and a certification in English as a second language (ESL). She was awarded a National Academy of Education/Spencer Post-doctoral Fellowship in 2025. Bunch has been an educator for 18+ years, and she is the founder of the un/HUSH teaching framework. You can learn more about her work at www.marleebunch.com.

Brittany R. Collins, MEd is an author, educator, and curriculum designer dedicated to promoting the social and emotional wellness of students and teachers. She is the author of *Learning From Loss: A Trauma-Informed Approach to Supporting Grieving Students*, as well as 70+ articles in outlets such as *The Washington Post, The Boston Globe, Education Week, The Hechinger Report, Inside Higher Ed*, and more. For two years, she worked as a contributing editor at Edutopia, where she enjoyed learning with and from teacher-writers. Currently, Brittany serves as the Director of Education at Write the World, a nonprofit dedicated to closing opportunity gaps in literacy education worldwide. She has also created curricula and educational programming for students and teachers through Harvard Graduate School of Education, Columbia University, PBS Learning Media, New York University, Smith College, Boston University, School Crisis Recovery and Renewal, and Race Project Kansas City, among other schools and organizations. She holds an MEd in curriculum and instruction, social-emotional learning, from the University of Virginia, as well as a certificate in trauma studies from the Trauma Research Foundation. Learn more about her work at www.brittanyrcollins.com.

Acknowledgments

Acknowledgments From Dr. Marlee S. Bunch

Special thanks and appreciation to Damian, Bella, Townes, and Aiden. You are the light of my life. Thank you, Mama, Jordan, and V for being my forever family. There are not adequate words to express my love and appreciation for having you in my life.

- Damian: Thank you for being my soldier and for your bright love. I am so lucky.
- Bella: You are my sunshine always, full of wonder and love.
- Townes: You are my freedom fighter extraordinaire, always loyal and compassionate.
- Aiden: You are my superhero—strong, kind, and curious. Being a Mama to the three of you has been the most meaningful part of my life.
- Bella B. and Dom: You are both so loved.
- Mama: Thank you for being the best Mama and Gigi, and bringing such joy to our lives. Your unconditional love fills my world.
- Grandmom: Thank you for your love and inspiration. You are my sunshine forever, and there is not a day that I do not miss you.
- To my family and friends: I am grateful every single day for your presence and support. I love and appreciate you beyond measure.
- Brittany: Thank you for your friendship and for all of the moments that have created the ability to laugh and dream. I think of all the times we have talked about writing together, so this feels like a dream come true. Collaborating

with you is always a gift, and I am so grateful our paths met once upon a summer day at Smith. We are Frick and Frack always.

I extend my appreciation and gratitude to the mentors and colleagues who have guided and supported me.

To ancestors and elders, I strive to honor your memory every day.

To my former students, who I learned so much from throughout the years. Being in a classroom with you was everything.

To the poets, artists, and creatives who keep our classroom and world human and full of imagination, thank you.

Thank you to Daniel and Routledge Press for your support and insights.

Jordan Stempleman and Emily Pettit, we are honored to include your work. Thank you for contributing your artistry and poetry. Your gift of words adds a humanness to this book that we are excited to share with others.

Much gratitude to Dr. Fay Cobb Payton. Your leadership, knowledge, and dedication in this space is so important. We are grateful for your willingness to collaborate and share your insights in the Foreword.

Cameron, thank you for contributing. Having your voice represented in this book is so meaningful.

Finally, thank you to all of the educators working to keep classrooms human-centered, culturally responsive, and full of joy.

Acknowledgments From Brittany R. Collins

When I write, I need solitude—I need quiet. On the best days, I escape to a coastline and let the crest of waves calm my mind, prepare it for work. Other times, it's a library nook or the furthest corner of my home. I need this because, in silence, the voices of so many others emerge—those from whom I've learned, who believed in me enough to push my thinking. Those for whom I "pay it forward."

How wonderful to co-author a book with one of those people; thank you, Marlee, for your friendship, collaboration, and creativity in this project and beyond.

To the teachers and mentors who inspired me at Campus School, the Williston Northampton School, Smith College, Holyoke Community College, Greenfield Community College, UMass Amherst, and the University of Virginia, you helped me pursue education no matter the odds.

To my colleagues, current and former, at Write the World, Inc. and Edutopia; my students at Harvard and Columbia; the teachers and administrators I've had the privilege of connecting with through grief-responsive professional development.

To those who make me laugh: Kerri, Tyla, Henry, Fabi, Katri, Sarah, Emma, Tierney, Ann, Marissa, the Zarbergs.

To those who listen.

And to my family: Mom, Grammy, and—in memory—Dad, Boppa, Grandma, Tom. Carpe diem.

Finally, to those who contributed their time and wisdom to this text: Dr. Fay Cobb Payton, Cameron Alleyne, Jordan Stempleman, Emily Pettit, and Daniel Schwartz and the Routledge team for carrying this work forward. I thank you.

Introduction

Marlee S. Bunch

Whether we like it or not, AI is here, and it will undoubtedly impact education and our classrooms for decades to come. The concerns around it are many. After all, AI is connected to systems that have perpetuated inequitable outcomes for marginalized people. Because AI tools are created by humans, they are susceptible to bias—gender bias, racial bias, and so forth. Humans who create the data that AI is trained on are subject to bias, which means that AI inevitably inherits it. Centuries of systemic inequities in education, healthcare, housing, banking, and so forth can be perpetuated and/or exacerbated by AI biases. For example, recent research has shown that the images generated by AI are typically white and male, and things such as darker skin tones are not detected by facial recognition. These examples illustrate only a few of the biases and inaccuracies that we must be acutely aware of.

> The quintessential problem is that the information we feed the machines reflects the biases and inequalities in our own society. Machines on their own are not racist or sexist, but if we give them biased data or algorithms, their decisions will amplify discrimination. There are really two causes for algorithmic bias: (1) historical human biases and (2) unrepresentative or incomplete training data and algorithms... We need to recognize and combat these biases to prevent discrimination and racist actions by machines that will likely be a large part of our future.
> (Lebovitz et al., 2021)

Being trained on primarily Western and white data leaves little room for the perspectives of our diverse world and can lead to the perpetuation of current misinformation or prejudices. Recent research such as that by Dr. Joy Buolamwini further illustrates and examines this bias. Building an understanding and awareness of this reality before delving into AI is imperative, as bias and a lack of cultural perspective are two flaws in current AI systems. We will examine this further in forthcoming chapters.

AI concerns are vast; AI has the ability to steal artwork, trick us into believing inaccurate information, create further divides regarding access to technology (e.g., in underfunded schools or rural areas), create inaccuracies in medical summaries, and perpetuate the many racial and socioeconomic inequities that AI is historically associated with. On paper, AI looks as if it will likely pose many concerns for society and our classrooms, specifically in the areas of equity and safety. There are valid concerns and hesitations related to how this quickly emerging world will allow teachers to maintain aspects of teaching that matter to all of us—helping students reach their highest potential, building relationships, encouraging academic and personal growth, and so forth. Policies and guidelines are needed to help manage the overall scope of AI, and as educators, we must begin to consider and inquire about ways that we can use AI as a tool that moves us toward innovation and access rather than widening the gaps (Rumale Vishwanath et al., 2024).

We must ask ourselves, How can we as educators work to maintain the human aspects of teaching and of the classroom that matter to our craft and the students we teach? There are an abundance of unknowns about AI, its capabilities, and what it will evolve into and look like in the future. However, we do know that AI makes mistakes, that it can mislead us and make us assume that we have accurate information. AI is like an unreliable narrator. Much like a character we come to love but who is unreliable, we never quite know what plot twists will emerge because of the character's actions. Sometimes, even at the end of the novel, we are still uncertain about what was entirely true and what was not, but nonetheless, we appreciate the character who led us through the journey. In the same way we navigate reading a book and getting to know a character who is unreliable, we must approach AI and teach our students to engage in the journey with us. Charting through unknown territories is something we as educators know how to do well, so hopefully we can find a way to be at the forefront of leading **how** AI is used in classrooms and schools so that we leverage its benefits for students and put guardrails into place to protect the aspects of learning that we know must remain. As Kahn (2024) notes, "AI can grant us all superpowers, if we make the right design choices and adopt the right policies" (pp. 5–6).

Our Story

Our story is a tapestry of lived experiences, lessons, and two educators coming together through collaboration and friendship. Because our story in many ways connects to the themes and topics we will explore in this book, I would like to take a moment to share a bit of our collective story with you. Brittany and I met in the summer of 2015 at Smith College. I was a mid-career educator and had taught primarily secondary English and writing courses. I had put myself through college, obtaining two master's degrees, an ESL (English as a second language) certification, and a Certificate in Gifted and Talented Education to help better understand and meet the needs of the varying degrees of academic readiness in my classroom. And yet, despite the many ways I had prepared myself to be a strong educator, something seemed to be missing, and little did I know, I would find it that summer. I was teaching a creative writing class, and Brittany was the teaching assistant assigned to the class. We instantly connected, and though Brittany was still in her teaching program, I asked her to embark on the class with me as a co-educator. We were Frick and Frack—seemingly different but similar and connected in ways we had not even yet realized. We collaborated on assignments, curriculum, and everything related to the class. We had a shared love of books, poetry, creativity, and the idea of making this world a little better through the work we would do with students. We used our lunchtime to brainstorm, assess, reflect, dream, and build our own relationship. Students often commented about the manner in which our collaborative efforts were obvious, and many students believed that we had known each other for many years. The approach we had toward the class and our practice was human-centered. We used creativity, dialogue, and unique assignments to create student investment and build a learning space that was academically and socially impactful. Our classroom was full of students from across the country—they were all young women, open-minded and willing to journey through the summer course with us. By the end of the course, they had written, analyzed, connected, created. By summer's end, I realized that what had been missing from my previous teaching was the collaborative teaching that Brittany and I had shared as we watched students hone their writing craft, share stories, and build relationships. Now, years later, despite all that has transpired in the world and in our own lives, the lasting memory of that summer remains, as does the friendship and collaborative partnership we established. Meaningful learning will always be what creates long-term impact. Whenever I approach a concern in pedagogy that feels insurmountable, I am reminded of that summer and the ways in which true collaboration can guide us through the hurdles we may encounter. Our connection, our ability to effectively collaborate, and the moments of clarity and hope that have emerged from the many questions related to teaching we have grappled with are all ultimately rooted in our collective story and in the intersectionality and interconnectedness that comes from our lived experiences. Effective collaboration for us has included listening, the ability to be vulnerable with each other, and the willingness to learn from each other (see Figure 0.1). We have collaborated

COLLABORATION & BEING IN COMMUNITY

By Dr. Marlee S. Bunch & Brittany R. Collins

1: GOOD PARTNERSHIPS

Good partnerships can create the following benefits:
- Challenge and expand our thinking
- Allow us to use our areas of expertise, while learning from someone else
- Build community and relationships
- Confront discomfort
- Unearth half-formed thoughts

2: CHARACTERISTICS

Characteristics of good collaboration include:
- Active listening
- Ability to have fun
- Vulnerability and honesty
- Mutual respect
- Shared purpose/goals
- Aspects that challenge our thinking/growth
- Open-mindedness
- Ability to safely disagree

3: REFLECT AND CONSIDER

With whom have you collaborated well with in the past? What energy do you bring to a collaboration? What type of energy do you need? What qualities do you contribute to a partnership? What do you most value in a collaborator? What lessons might you hope to learn? What might you hope to unlearn?

4. SELF-WORK

Collaboration asks us to unlearn and relearn. Self-work precedes the ability to effectively collaborate. Self-work may look like:
- Practicing freewriting or journaling
- Processing and sharing challenging stories
- Going to therapy
- Sharing honest feedback with a peer
- Identifying and advocating for your needs
- Letting go of performativity or perfectionism
- Understanding where your beliefs and emotional reactions come from

5. HEALING

Self-work and collaboration involve healing. In partnership, this may look like:
- Naming and sharing honest emotions and reactions
- Asking open-ended questions
- Communicating needs and boundaries
- Discussing your working relationship in addition to the work involved
- Identifying and complementing each other's strengths and areas for growth
- Sharing the work equitably

> "One of the most vital ways we sustain ourselves is by building communities of resistance, places where we know we are not alone."
> ~ bell hooks

FIGURE 0.1 Collaboration and Being in Community

through our different lived experiences, racial identities, and our teaching approaches—leading us to work together on writing, curricula, and editing; have hard conversations; and celebrate each other's accomplishments. Our meeting, in and of itself, illustrates that stories have the power to connect and that collective efforts toward learning and evolving yield positive results for everyone involved. We believe that collaboration is one of the most culturally responsive, human, and powerful tools educators have. We are excited to begin this journey with you, the reader, as we consider, question and walk through the unknowns of AI together and create tools for our classrooms and learning spaces.

Beliefs and Hopes

We believe that language and connection are our greatest powers. At the end of our summer Smith course, Brittany and I compiled and created a book of the class writing that students had produced—poems, short stories, and essays. As our students at Smith worked to compile our end-of-the-term collection of writing, and we witnessed them collaborating and becoming excited and engaged in the writing they had created, we recognized the power of its potential. The class titled it "The Safest Place You Can Be," a memory now that reminds me of the power of human connection and the possibilities that can occur when we create spaces that are open, challenging, and invested in our students' academic and emotional growth. That simple photocopied collection of writing, which featured images of our students on the front cover, spoke to how human connectedness can create safety and a place where learning can thrive.

From oral histories to written narratives, to truths whispered to a friend, we believe that stories are foundational to understanding the self and others—to creating equitable, healing-centered classrooms that focus on the lived experiences and holistic identities of students. What drives our commitment and hope regarding education is the students and the stories they bring to the classroom. What are your fundamental beliefs and hopes about your classroom? Education? Students?

Taking a moment to identify those is a great way to begin this book. We believe that reflection, journaling, and putting pen to paper help to center our intentions and provide clarity. We invite you to take a moment now to consider the questions and sentiments presented. Understanding our beliefs and what drives our classrooms helps set the foundation for how we choose to approach new and emerging elements that ultimately impact teaching and learning.

Origin Story

This book was born out of the questions and musings of two friends, late one evening, as we began discussing new ways that artificial intelligence (AI) was being used in education and the concerns we had related to it. Like many educators, we wonder how it will impact our classrooms, what will be lost with AI advancements, and how we can work to successfully incorporate it in classrooms so that students have guidance as they navigate this rapidly changing world. Since our time at Smith, Brittany and I have continued our teaching endeavors and our commitment to creating culturally responsive learning spaces. My primary focus has been on culturally responsive and community-immersive classrooms, and Brittany has focused on the intersections of trauma-informed education, grief-responsive teaching, disability advocacy, and equity-centered social-emotional learning. Sometimes referred to as transformative social-emotional learning (TSEL), this approach takes a systems-based perspective on youth and educator well-being. Our intersections of interest and the ways our differences complement one another convinced us that our joint experiences will offer you (the reader) varied and rich perspectives. My most recent learning endeavors included completing my doctoral degree at the University of Illinois in education/policy/organizational leadership and completing my first books, *The Magnitude of Us: An Educator's Guide* to *Creating Culturally Responsive Classrooms* (Teachers College Press, 2024) and *Unlearning the Hush: Oral Histories of Black Female Educators in Mississippi in the Civil Rights Era* (University of Illinois Press, 2025). And Brittany recently completed her MEd in curriculum and instruction, with a focus on social-emotional learning (SEL), from the University of Virginia, after publishing *Learning From Loss: A Trauma-Informed Approach to Supporting Grieving Students* (Collins, 2021) and earning a certificate in traumatic stress studies from the Trauma Research Foundation.

AI is new territory for us, and it took our individual and joint exploration to begin making sense of some of the new things emerging from the AI world. We have no formal background or training in technology or AI, and we share many of the same concerns that others do regarding the merging of AI and education. As educators, we often discuss concerns related to issues that will impact our field, and this topic was no different. We decided to walk through some of our concerns together. Over Zoom, we shared and discussed our concerns and then decided to see what would happen if we asked AI to create a lesson plan regarding topics we were familiar with. Experimenting in this way allowed us to begin thinking through some of the worries we had voiced and to evaluate both the benefits and downsides of AI.

We started by asking AI general questions about various topics we are knowledgeable about and were impressed by the answers it returned. However, we quickly realized that the more specific the questions, the less accurate the responses. It was at that moment that we began to realize that while AI was an intuitive tool, it lacked the ability to fill in details and specifics that would occur through research, with a mentor, in a classroom with a good instructor, and so on. This allowed us to breathe a sigh of relief. However, we acknowledge that AI is rapidly evolving and improving, so these limitations may change in the near future. We are just witnessing the beginning of AI, but we are certain that the power of relationships and good pedagogy will always be the best ways to inform learning and connection. Ultimately, the core beliefs that solidified our friendship and collaboration—storytelling and questions, inquiry and discussions—were the very elements that we knew would be the answer to the conundrums and concerns regarding AI in the classroom. The human aspect of learning is the key to drawing a line in the sand between AI capabilities and good teaching.

Significance

AI is a vast topic, and there are undoubtedly many, many unknowns. Like you, we are beginning to try to make sense of what it entails, consider what some of the benefits are, evaluate and examine the concerns, and navigate how to incorporate AI into the classroom in equitable ways. AI and its many unknowns and complexities are both scary and intriguing, and we recognize the need for educators to begin learning about it so we can best discern how it will impact our students, classrooms, and pedagogy. At this very moment, there is much to be concerned about in education and society: teacher shortages; inequities in education; soaring gun violence in schools and beyond; book bans; a youth mental health crisis; the removal or restriction of history in classrooms; proposed legislation attempting to ban SEL and diversity, equity, and inclusion programs; the potential dismantling of the U.S. Department of Education; and much more. At a time when humanity is so needed, we wanted to help other educators begin to make sense of AI and find applicable ways to use it in a manner that aligns with culturally responsive classrooms. Rather than focus on how AI might perpetuate academic dishonesty or debate in a binary way whether students should or should not be using it, we wanted to offer some of the ways that we might leverage AI to enhance good pedagogy. Given the perils of AI if used incorrectly or in a manner that is uninformed, bringing AI into the classroom requires examining the downsides and concerns so we can discover how to use it as a potential tool, in a manner that supports cultural responsiveness and deep learning. The more we as educators experiment and understand AI, the better positioned we are to guide students in their use of AI. In the chapters ahead, you will find graphics, stories, personal narratives, reflection questions, and guiding tools, with culturally responsive teaching and social-emotional learning threaded throughout. This book marks the importance of continuous learning and a willingness to jump into the unknown to question, fumble, and discover collectively. We invite you to join us as we embark upon this journey.

The Perils of AI

We want to acknowledge upfront that AI has many unknowns and possible perils, and those concerns continue to grow as AI evolves. Even since this book went to print, advancements occurred that we could not be aware of while writing. We know that the changes and advancements of AI are vast and move quickly. Not only can AI be inaccurate, but it can also perpetuate broad misunderstandings and prejudices about everything from gender to race (Lifshitz et al., 2021). AI can be biased and work against some of the principles of culturally responsive teaching that many of us are trying to embed in our classrooms. Additionally, students becoming dependent on AI for information means that they could lose the development of important critical thinking skills, analysis, and inquiry—all necessities for college readiness and life. Finally, of course, as educators, we do not want to fill our students' learning and minds with the falsehoods and misinformation that AI has the potential to generate. Therefore, we need to be aware of its failings and shortfalls so that we can prepare to help students both mine AI for its valuable tools and beware of where it might present information that is inaccurate or biased. More recently, research is indicating that when

AI is trained on the content it creates, it becomes worse and even more problematic. A higher degree of errors and content pollution can occur when AI ingests its own content. Simply stated, when AI makes a copy of itself, and then another copy, followed by more copies, the end result and output is often unrecognizable from the original text or image. Think about how an original photo looks after being placed in a brochure that someone makes a copy of. Once copied multiple times, the original clarity is lost, and the brochure image ends up looking muddled and distorted. "The model becomes poisoned with its own projection of reality," researchers wrote of this phenomenon (Bhatia, 2024). This problem isn't just confined to text. Another team of researchers at Rice University studied what would happen when the kinds of AI that generate images are repeatedly trained on their own output—"a problem that could already be occurring as AI-generated images flood the web" (Bhatia, 2024). These types of errors and distortions ultimately greatly impact the information we find on the web and, particularly, skew data. "Studies have found that this process can amplify biases in the data and is more likely to erase data pertaining to minorities" (Bhatia, 2024). Because many of the language models do not have access to peer-reviewed databases, it is difficult to discern credibility and quality data. This means that research and data found online are even more susceptible to errors and misinformation, especially information related to marginalized people and communities.

If these concerns are not enough, it is also worth acknowledging that AI presents pitfalls for educators, too, some of which will challenge our teaching practices and encourage us to be better sleuths for detecting misinformation. AI challenges will require us to expand our craft, increase our knowledge base, be better researchers and planners, and be committed to teaching in a manner that is both culturally responsive and responsive to students' social and emotional needs. This undoubtedly is hard work, but it's imperative and beneficial. Finally, we recognize that AI presents ways for students to potentially be academically dishonest or take academic shortcuts. However, rather than approaching AI as merely a tool for cheating, we want to invite you to consider that if used intentionally and with an acute awareness of its pitfalls, AI has the potential to be more than just negative.

The good news is that recent advancements in algorithmic accountability (including the introduction of the Algorithmic Accountability Act of 2019), data minimization policies (rules that prevent harmful data collection), and privacy regulations all work to improve areas of AI that need reform (Library of Congress, n.d.). Many researchers, educators, and organizations are committed to ensuring accountability and equity related to AI (e.g., the Ida B. Wells Just Data Lab, the Algorithmic Justice League, MediaJustice, and the AI Now Institute). As educators, we can support these larger efforts and help students learn how to use AI in a responsible and discerning manner, just as we do with academic content. Being aware of the perils related to AI can help us grow as educators, open up new approaches to learning for our students, and help us find tools to pair with other good teaching practices that we know will always be foundational to inquiry-based classrooms. The good news and upside to the perils involved with AI is that they remind us that good research and high-quality teaching are difficult to replicate or replace, even for artificial intelligence models and systems. I recently read an article comparing AI to a microwave (Marche, 2024): While useful, it cannot do everything. Rarely do we opt to microwave a grilled cheese sandwich. The original method of making it cannot be replaced. The author shares,

> The writing that matters, the writing that we are going to have to start teaching, is grilled cheese writing—the kind that only humans can create: writing with less performance and more originality . . . The ideas that people want are still handmade.
>
> (Marche, 2024)

For now, the human elements that exist in classrooms and within the art of teaching will remain valuable and necessary for both education and the benefit of students.

Roadmap

As you delve into the book, you will find that we have attempted to include other perspectives and voices—you will see that each chapter is followed by a poetic reflection (a nod to our love of language and the importance of creativity in the classroom, and a trademark of my [Bunch's] research, as we cannot think of a more human-centered act than that of crafting an original poem and being open to the world of language and reflection in the way that poetry encourages us to do). Though often underutilized in the classroom, poems remind us of the importance of relational learning and of the human-centered storytelling at the heart of our pedagogy. Perhaps these poems will invite you to try poetry in your classroom or engage with it personally. After all, teaching itself is a creative act, one that ties easily to the humanity that poetry represents. Jordan Stempleman, the poet and educator who wrote the poems, shared, "The poems speak of the tradeoffs and the limitations of all forms of communication and critical thought, and how these various language systems interact with the world and one's mind." The poems included in the book are connected to the idea of maintaining and discovering the most human elements of ourselves and our learning. What we appreciate about poetry, and art in general, is its ability to encourage dialogue, foster cross-cultural appreciation, and give us space to grapple with the unknown. There are no immediate answers, and engaging with art requires patience and a willingness to listen—the embodiment of culturally responsive teaching and human-centered learning. In Chapter 4, you'll find writing prompts that inspire your students to engage with these poems directly and to use AI as a meaningful tool in their own authentic writing processes. Remaining grounded (to use a word from one of Stempleman's poems) in what matters is what we believe is most essential to teaching and learning: building relationships and creating meaningful points for inquiry and curiosity.

We hope the poems and creative thinking offer an entry point for reflection and pause, again anchoring us in the humanness of teaching and connecting with others. Because we also believe that amplifying student voices is always important, we have included an Afterword written by a high school student, Cameron Alleyne, with whom Brittany worked at the nonprofit Write the World, Inc. Collaborating and sharing diverse perspectives is integral to our own collaborative work. You will also notice that we will use personal narratives and stories, including bylines in each chapter to ensure you know who is speaking. This blend of guidebook-meets-narrative represents our commitment to using stories and personal connection in the classroom and as collaborators.

We've placed an AI symbol above any content that was generated by AI so that it is easy to discern what is our writing and what are the results of our exploring various AI tools. Chapter 1 offers a broad-brush overview of emerging AI technologies—what they are, the types of tools that are emerging, and how they are most relevant to teachers. If you're already an AI aficionado, you might skip to Chapter 2, which offers a guide for creating culturally responsive classrooms while working alongside AI. Chapter 3 looks at how we can use AI tools to enhance social-emotional learning (SEL), cultivating in students five core SEL competencies. Chapter 4 weaves together these human-centered pedagogies—SEL and culturally responsive teaching—applying them to the English language arts (ELA) classroom and considering strategies for using AI in ELA to advance these two types of teaching. Finally, Chapter 5 shares an overview of ways to use AI to enhance history and social studies.

Throughout the book, you will also encounter charts, guides, activities, and other pedagogical tools such as "Stop and Think" sections that invite you to pause and reflect on the contents of each chapter and how you might apply your learnings to practice. Additionally, every chapter concludes with a "Try Out the Tech and Reflect" section that invites you to experiment with AI technologies and document your thinking. Finally, the appendices offer additional resources and reflection prompts for extended learning. While there are many resources for incorporating AI into classrooms, few address culturally responsive teaching and social-emotional learning. The road to understanding how to use AI in the classroom is not yet fleshed out or wholly understood, but we hope that by the end of this book, you will feel more at ease with the idea of incorporating and addressing some of the approaching realities of AI in learning spaces.

Let's begin . . .

References

Bhatia, A. (2024, August 26). When A.I.'s output is a threat to A.I. itself. *The New York Times*. www.nytimes.com/interactive/2024/08/26/upshot/ai-synthetic-data.html

Buolamwini, J. (2024). *Unmasking AI: My mission to protect what is human in a world of machines*. Random House.

Collins, B. R. (2021). *Learning from loss: A trauma-informed approach to supporting grieving students*. Heinemann.

Kahn, J. (2024). *Mastering AI*. Simon and Schuster.

Lebovitz, S., Levina, N., & Lifshitz-Assa, H. (2021). Is AI ground truth really true? The dangers of training and evaluating AI tools based on experts' know-what. *MIS Quarterly*, *45*(3), 1501–1526. https://doi.org/10.25300/misq/2021/16564

Library of Congress. (n.d.). All information (except text) for H.R.2231 - Algorithmic Accountability Act of 2019. 116th Congress (2019–2020). Congress.gov. www.congress.gov/bill/116th-congress/house-bill/2231/all-info

Lifshitz, B., Maldonado, V., Nlekkas, Chkhartishvili, T., ONeil, A., Editors, G., Benson, S., LaRivee, W., Hardesty, E., Ramakrishnan, A., Dunlevie, T.,

Bernd, L., Herlihy, J., Hempel, P., Kunkle, W., Wooley, S., Durland, H., Bergman, L., Cope, S., . . . Dorshow, A. (2021, May 6). Racism is systemic in artificial intelligence systems, too. *Georgetown Security Studies Review*. https://georgetownsecuritystudiesreview.org/2021/05/06/racism-is-systemic-in-artificial-intelligence-systems-too/#_edn15

Marche, S. (2024, September 27). AI is a language microwave. *The Atlantic*. https://www.theatlantic.com/technology/archive/2024/09/ai-language-microwave/680049/

Rumale Vishwanath, P., Tiwari, S., Naik, T. G., Gupta, S., Thai, D. N., Zhao, W., Kwon, S., Ardulov, V., Tarabishy, K., McCallum, A., & Salloum, W. (2024). Faithfulness hallucination detection in healthcare AI. In *Proceedings of KDD-AIDSH 2024*, August 26, 2024, Barcelona, Spain. https://openreview.net/pdf?id=6eMIzKFOpJ

Poetic Reflection

Grounded Generation

Jordan Stempleman

Here is a prediction.
This is well past the start

of something.
There is another aloneness

somewhat unlike us, churning
around the clock.

There is a language
of people, kind of not,

but willing. Something
we are made of, the let-out

wandering, becoming us
as we put it to mind.

Today, I'm being called
by the similar

and the estranged
at once.

I am ready to turn toward
the better matters

not yet understood.
The afternoon

before I thought
of this afternoon

was me, wasn't it?
As I found it,

I was moved.
The world begins and ends

in what we welcome, how far
we are taken.

1

What Is AI, Anyway? An Overview for Educators

Brittany R. Collins

When I first logged onto the ChatGPT website one warm afternoon in the spring of 2023, several metaphors came to mind: I felt, on one hand, like Doctor Who flying his spaceship, the TARDIS, through galaxies unknown, on a quest to do good—to save as many aliens or earthlings as he could in the face of evil.

The middle school students I've worked with would have liked this comparison.

On the other hand, however, I imagined the antagonists against which the television hero often fought—larger than life robots turned sentient, ready to take over the planet. Would AI technology be more like a TARDIS or a traitor—the first step toward a superintelligence that could conquer us all? Would those using it leverage its power more for harm or for healthy—even transformative—innovation? And what are the implications of AI, not only for academic learning in the classroom, but for deeply relational pedagogies, such as culturally responsive teaching and social-emotional learning, that until now have been defined by their humanness: Would generative artificial intelligence dampen, replace, or somehow sideline these heart-centric approaches to teaching and learning?

Setting aside what may seem like a puerile comparison to a popular television show, these central inquiries have become, in less than 12 months at the time of my writing this, more prescient than many of us could have imagined. And their answers are, collectively, ours for the writing. In the last year alone, we have watched as school districts banned what seemed, to many, like an unethical technology—one that could spark student plagiarism at scale, in undetectable ways. Yet merely one summer vacation later, in September, 2023, many of those same schools repealed their bans (Singer, 2023), citing workforce readiness, technology integration, 21st-century learning skills, and equity issues; students who lack access to technology at home, for example, have limited exposure to these emerging, and likely enduring, tools, and that disparity could deepen the "digital divide" (Choi & Handjojo, 2023) that became even more vivid during the COVID-19 pandemic. We therefore need, districts claimed, to not only face but learn how best to leverage that which initially seemed to many like a superfluous, if not immoral, technology.

Fast forward, and it's now hard to log on to any education, technology, literacy, or news website and *not* find mention of AI within the first few clicks or scrolls. Educational AI tools abound, with platforms like MagicSchool, SchoolAI, Khan Academy's Khanmigo, the International Society for Technology in Education (ISTE)'s StretchAI, and Eduaide being just some of the names that have dominated the teaching and learning landscape of late (by the time you read this, even these tools might seem like fossils). But the nuts and bolts of the technology remain elusive for many—even AI researchers are finding its behavior mysterious (Heaven, 2024). In 2024, a survey of 1,020 U.S. public school teachers showed that only 15% had used AI in the classroom, though "60% of school districts [planned] to train teachers about AI use by the end of the 2023–24 school year, according to the Rand-CRPE findings" (Merod, 2024, p. 1). Notably, "urban school districts were the least likely to plan such training"

(p. 1), implicating a number of the equity-related inquiries we'll explore in chapters to come.

But although AI may seem, in many ways, like breaking news, it is not truly novel, having been in development, and at the heart of governmental, scientific, and academic debates, for decades.

This begs us to ask, "What is AI, anyway?"

In this chapter, we share a high-level overview of what, exactly, this "emerging" technology is, how it came to dominate the tech landscape in this seemingly short time span, and the most common functionalities it offers as related to teaching and learning. We also paint in broad brushstrokes some of the, ethical, equity, and moral concerns that implicate educators which we will explore with greater depth in chapters to come. We present a call for a new type of critical thinking—that competency at the core of so much of our work in education— that takes AI into account in our work with young people and invites them into the conversation, not as passive recipients of educators' edicts about this technology but as active participants in the co-construction of community values and norms regarding its uses—as analyzers, "de-coders," if you will, of both its perils and potentials—true to a constructivist approach to teaching and learning (in which, now, AI is positioned as a collaborator in the construction of knowledge, not an omniscient replacement for the deep, iterative processes of idea-building and inquiry).

Box 1.1 💡 Stop and Think

What do you already know about what AI is and how it works? What questions do you have about these technologies? How did you feel when you first learned about AI, and why? Have your feelings changed across time? Why or why not? What do you view as the powers and potential perils—the pros and cons—of these technological tools?

What Is AI?

Though artificial intelligence may seem brand new, it has a long and vivid history not often captured in current news coverage. As I wrote in an historical overview of AI for Write the World, Inc., a writing education nonprofit where I work with middle and high school students and teachers:

> The idea of robots or other forms of technology emulating human intelligence spans back to science fiction (demonstrating the power of writing!) produced as early as 1938—and the first pioneering paper on AI technology, titled "Can Machines Think?," was produced by Alan Turing in 1950.
>
> In that paper, Turing posed a pivotal question; he "suggested that humans use available information as well as reason in order to solve problems and make decisions, so why can't machines do the same thing?" That inquiry sparked a flurry of scientific interest and investment in artificial intelligence technologies, which have ebbed and flowed ever since; at root, technologists, engineers, and others have worked to answer Turing's question, creating computer systems that mimic the way the human brain works.
>
> (Collins, 2024, p. 1)

This notion of emulating how the human brain works feels especially relevant for educators. Technologists are, in essence, trying to replicate the very thing we engage in every day—the learning, knowledge-building, and relational processes that students, teachers, curriculum designers, and administrators facilitate every time they are together in a learning environment. Engineers call this "deep learning."

As educators, we already know a thing or two about that.

Generative Artificial Intelligence

Let's explore some common terms appearing across the AI world right now. First, **generative AI** is artificial intelligence that can produce (think *generate*) content, like text, images, and video. ChatGPT, one of the most popular and commonplace artificial intelligence tools at the moment, is a generative large language model. In generative AI, the technology is trained on large sets of unstructured human-generated data, like text published publicly on the Internet or in libraries of stock images. That's the process of **deep learning**:

> Deep learning is a method in artificial intelligence (AI) that teaches computers to process data in a way that is inspired by the human brain. Deep learning models can recognize complex patterns in pictures, text, sounds, and other data to produce accurate insights and predictions.
> (Amazon Web Services, 2024, p. 1)

As educators, we know that the human brain undergoes many complex processes when learning. So does artificial intelligence technology. In deep learning, **neural networks** "mimic how neurons in the brain signal one another . . . [and] are made up of node layers—an input layer, one or more hidden layers, and an output layer" (IBM Data & AI Team, 2024, p. 1). This process is quite complex, and it's not necessarily essential for you to fully understand it in order to apply AI in meaningful, responsible, responsive ways in the classroom. But for those who are excited by the technological specifics of these tools, we've included in the appendices more reading related to this topic.

What is important to know about deep learning, though, is that—in essence—**statistics and probability** are at play; the technology—and again, this is a highly simplistic description—is trained, in phases, to notice patterns in data and to internalize those patterns enough to generate content that is the most statistically probable fit for the input (e.g., prompt) that it receives. So, if I were prompting ChatGPT or MagicSchool to create a lesson plan to teach 10th-graders about the Civil War, the tools—**large language models, or LLMs**, which respond to and create text—have been trained on content publicly available on the Internet and will generate the most statistically probable output, like the outline of a lesson plan that touches on the key names, dates, and historical figures involved in the conflict, based on the words that I include in my prompt.

This dance between input and output can further hone the accuracy and usefulness of the results—as in conversation, we go deeper the more we interact, and so is the case between AI and humans.

Terminology and Foundational Information

There are many terms in the world of AI; throughout this book, we do our best to use those most familiar and applicable to teachers. As you read, feel free to return to Figure 1.1, which offers the definitions of key words and phrases related to AI.

Types of Generative AI Tools

Generative AI tools that deal in language, as noted before, are large language models, but even within the world of LLMs, there are many different types of tools relevant to the classroom and different use cases for them (Collins, 2024). Additionally, there are generative AI tools beyond LLMs that deal with multimedia. Some refer to these as large multimodal models, or LMMs (Guinness, 2024), though the acronym is also used to describe large medical models, which are trained on medical data, so we'll refrain from using it definitively here (Sahu, 2024).

We've grouped these different types of tools using our own categories, which you may also find helpful.

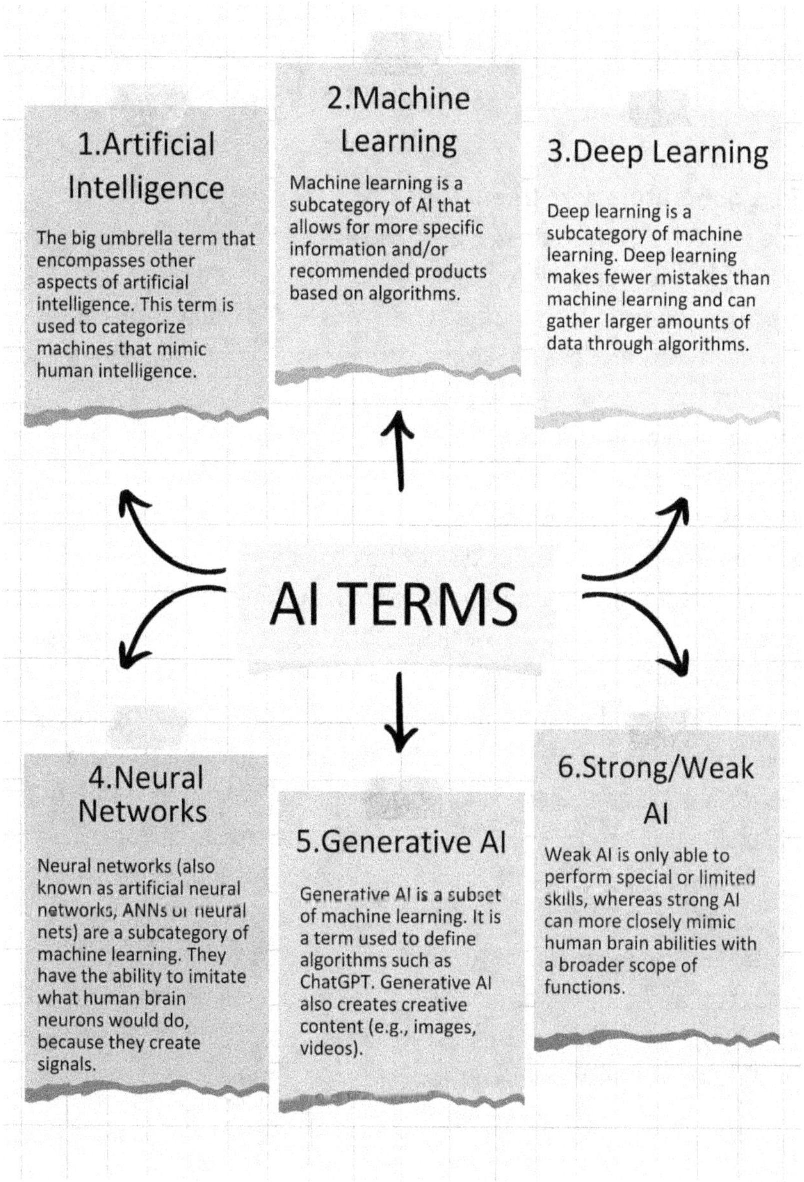

What Is AI, Anyway? An Overview for Educators ◆ 25

1. Artificial Intelligence

The big umbrella term that encompasses other aspects of artificial intelligence. This term is used to categorize machines that mimic human intelligence.

2. Machine Learning

Machine learning is a subcategory of AI that allows for more specific information and/or recommended products based on algorithms.

3. Deep Learning

Deep learning is a subcategory of machine learning. Deep learning makes fewer mistakes than machine learning and can gather larger amounts of data through algorithms.

AI TERMS

4. Neural Networks

Neural networks (also known as artificial neural networks, ANNs or neural nets) are a subcategory of machine learning. They have the ability to imitate what human brain neurons would do, because they create signals.

5. Generative AI

Generative AI is a subset of machine learning. It is a term used to define algorithms such as ChatGPT. Generative AI also creates creative content (e.g., images, videos).

6. Strong/Weak AI

Weak AI is only able to perform special or limited skills, whereas strong AI can more closely mimic human brain abilities with a broader scope of functions.

FIGURE 1.1 AI Terminology

Box 1.2 Types of AI Tools

Text generators. Like OpenAI's ChatGPT, text generators, or large language models, are generative AI tools that deal exclusively in text, responding to human words (input/prompt) with the most statistically probable words in turn (output). From answers to factual questions to poems, novels, and business memos, these tools create language-based content.

Image/video generators. These tools work similarly to LLMs in that they, too, require human input, but their output is multimodal, such as images, videos, or cartoons.

Personae. Another form of LLM is the character-based chatbot (which you can create and customize yourself in ChatGPT alone) that is prompted to take on the form of a specific persona. Some tools with preexisting personae exist, like Khan Academy's chatbot, Khanmigo, which is trained to respond to students as a tutor would, in a mostly Socratic fashion, with guiding questions rather than answers. Character.ai, another example, allows one to chat with fictional or historical characters. And teaching assistant chatbots, like ISTE and ASCD's StretchAI and MagicSchool's Raina, are positioned as pedagogical partners, responding to teachers as colleagues.

Collateral generators. We use this category to group together large language and multimodal models that create a variety of formulated content beyond just text, like tools for creating slides, grants, worksheets, quizzes, lesson plans, websites, professional résumés, and more.

Ethics and Equity Implications

Of course, as we begin to think about the role of these tools in culturally responsive teaching and social-emotional learning and apply them to English language arts and social studies curricula in chapters to come, it's critical to consider the ethics and equity issues that they pose—both those flaws that exist inherently in the (current) technology and in humans' uses of the technology. This may feel alarmist, but by examining and understanding the possible harms of these tools, we are better positioned to proactively leverage and use them for good.

Technological Concerns

Hallucinations

As educators, we know that errors are an inevitable part of students' learning. So, too, in AI's deep learning. When an error occurs—when AI produces false information or an incorrect answer—it's called a *hallucination*. Authors at IBM write that hallucinations are "a phenomenon wherein a large language model (LLM)—often a generative AI chatbot or computer vision tool—perceives patterns or objects that are nonexistent or imperceptible to human observers, creating outputs that are nonsensical or altogether inaccurate" (2023, p. 1). Hallucinations are not uncommon. As of November 2023, researchers found that AI systems from OpenAI, Meta, and Google made up information at rates of 3%, 5%, and 27%, respectively (Metz, 2023).

Biases

The human-generated data upon which AI is trained contain biases and stereotypes—a microcosm of the "-isms" that pervade our world, from racism to sexism to political ire to homophobia. "Scientists from MIT found that a language model thinks that 'flight attendant,' 'secretary,' and 'physician's assistant' are feminine jobs, while 'fisherman,' 'lawyer,' and 'judge' are masculine," writes Aniya Greene-Santos for the National Education Association. "Meanwhile, researchers at Dartmouth found language models that have biases, like stereotypes, baked into them.

Their findings suggested, for example, that a particular group of people are either good or bad at certain skills" (2024, p. 1). So, AI outputs may contain offensive and harmful biases and stereotypes and may influence the human recipient and, in turn, perpetuate those biases and stereotypes.

Tone and Inappropriate Content

Within the "personae" category of AI tools, there are chatbots trained to produce language in sarcastic or rude tones. There are also bots trained to create sexual and other content that would be inappropriate for youth. When we integrate AI into classroom settings, we therefore need to be mindful of the tools we use, the parameters we put around them, and the other tools or content students may find by way of that which we introduce. Our prompting can also place parameters on the types of content the tools produce with students, which we'll explore throughout the book—for example, we can set up ChatGPT personae that will only respond to students with open-ended questions, or with empathy and constructive criticism, or in a particular tone, voice, or style.

Human Use Concerns

Deepfakes

Deepfakes are images, videos, audio files, and other content pieces generated to represent someone's likeness—such as a celebrity saying something offensive in an ad that they never said in real life. Brooks et al. (n.d.) writes,

> The threat of Deepfakes and synthetic media comes not from the technology used to create it, but from

people's natural inclination to believe what they see, and as a result deepfakes and synthetic media do not need to be particularly advanced or believable in order to be effective in spreading mis/disinformation.

Because AI tools can produce images and videos portraying real people, deepfakes may proliferate in a way not previously possible with tools like Adobe Photoshop. And while there are legal ramifications for deepfakes, it may become harder and harder to identify them.

Equity Issue: Gender

So far in this chapter, we've highlighted gender discrimination in AI output and considered deepfakes; when considering gender equity issues related to AI, it's crucial to note that young women are more likely to be victimized by deepfake nudes, including those created by classmates, taking cyberbullying to a new level (this is illegal, considered child sexual abuse material, and must be reported). "A.I.-generated images to harass, humiliate and bully young women can harm their mental health, reputations and physical safety as well as pose risks to their college and career prospects," writes Natasha Singer for *The New York Times* (2024, p. 1). What's more, women will be disproportionately impacted by AI-related job losses (West, 2024). And "systems built on AI have exceptionally low rates of recognition for nonbinary people or other gender categories" (Uribe, 2024, p. 1).

Equity Issue: Race

Dr. Joy Buolamwini—pioneering artificial intelligence researcher, founder of the Algorithmic Justice League, and author of *Unmasking A.I.: My Mission to Protect What Is Human in a World of Machines*—coined the term "excoded" to describe "individuals or communities harmed by algorithmic systems" (2023a, p. 226). After realizing that she could code only while wearing a white mask due to inequities in facial recognition software, which were not trained on dark skin tones and thus cannot detect them, Buolamwini dedicated her career to calling attention to the ways in which AI technologies harm marginalized individuals and what we can all do to create more humane and responsive tech. She notes in her book that self-driving cars, which use AI, currently struggle to detect and stop for non-white bodies, demonstrating that technological inequities can have literal life-or-death ramifications (Buolamwini, 2023b). In 2024, a news feature published in *Nature* highlighted that AI image generators produced racist and sexist results (Ananya, 2024). AI tools used in the scanning of résumés, in surveillance technologies, in determining how much individuals pay for online merchandise, in credit scoring, and many other automatic processes across sectors all hold the potential to perpetuate racial and other discrimination with individual and systemic consequences (Buolamwini, 2018).

Authors at the American Civil Liberties Union (ACLU) write,

> AI tools have perpetuated housing discrimination, such as in tenant selection and mortgage qualifications, as well as hiring and financial lending discrimination. For example, AI systems used to evaluate potential tenants rely on court records and other datasets that have their own built-in biases that reflect systemic racism, sexism, and ableism, and are notoriously full of errors. People are regularly denied housing, despite

their ability to pay rent, because tenant screening algorithms deem them ineligible or unworthy.

(Akselrod, 2023, p. 1)

Generative AI tools, like LLMs, may also struggle to produce historically accurate content about marginalized individuals and communities, which we'll explore in chapters to come.

Equity Issue: Linguistic Diversity and English Language Learning

I was recently speaking with a colleague who shared that she rarely uses LLMs because, as someone for whom English is a second language, she finds that the tools do not accurately or authentically depict her accent, mannerisms, and other uses of language(s).

Her feelings are affirmed by research findings: "When writing tools prioritise one way of writing over another, they reinforce existing hierarchies that unfairly position Standard American English (SAE) and the Queen's English over other languages and ways of writing," writes Collin Bjork in *The Conversation* (2023, p. 1). Of course, such silencing is already present at school; Bjork adds,

> The decision to prioritise Standard American English in many US classrooms, for example, means that speakers of Black English a language with its own grammar, lexicon and remarkable history of resistance—are penalised and shamed for writing as they speak.
>
> (2023, p. 1)

Adding technology that further homogenizes language or superimposes a specific dialect threatens to widen this chasm. And while we can prompt AI tools to respond to us in a number of voices and tones, their authenticity remains up for questioning; tech companies are aware of this, recently adding more languages to AI tools but for translation purposes, which are different from capturing authentic dialects in output. The former use case, though, does raise the question of whether generative AI can serve as an English language learning support tool. Might teachers now be able to create content at multiple Lexile levels, for example, or invite students to use AI tools for grammar and mechanics support? Or perhaps they can create images to complement text, providing multiple modes of representation—thus fulfilling a critical tenet in the Universal Design for Learning framework (CAST, 2024). We'll explore these possibilities—for using AI to enhance differentiation within classrooms and curricula—in chapters to come.

The Need for a New Form of Critical Thinking

The many concerns threaded throughout this chapter, highlighting potential harms of AI tech and human uses of it, are just a starting place. You likely have many concerns of your own. But they are also a platform from which to build and innovate, allowing us to make educated decisions about how we intentionally and responsibly acquaint students with these tools and their pros and cons as well as how we support young people's digital literacy, critical literacy, and citizenship in and beyond the classroom.

I already mentioned the power of constructivist education—of engaging students in authentic inquiry as co-authors of new knowledge. As we progress throughout this book, we'll consider how to engage with youth directly about AI models, their ethics, perils, and sociopolitical implications, not as didactic rule-setters but as collaborators in this new journey. As AI natives, students' perspectives are essential; take, for instance, the voice of teen writer Shekina Oh from the Philippines, who wrote in an

AI-themed issue of the *Write the World Review*, an online literary journal for middle and high school students, that the

> . . . spoon-feeding nature of AI may promote passive learning, wherein students consume information instead of thinking through and analyzing it . . . Despite this weakness, AI may also facilitate learning through its accessibility to students, access to a wide range of resources, and personalized approach to users.
>
> (2024, p. 13)

As we set policies and establish how best to use AI in learning spaces, teens' voices can help lead the way.

Box 1.3 Try Out the Tech and Reflect

To apply learnings from this chapter, you might:

1. Find an article or resource regarding deepfakes or AI-related inequities that is appropriate to share with your students. Read the article with your class and engage in discussion using the "Take a Stand" thinking routine from Harvard Graduate School of Education's Project Zero, a framework that asks students to share their opinion, consider those of their peers, revise or hone their opinion, consider broader societal issues, and account for complicating scenarios as appropriate (Project Zero & Common Sense Media, 2021, p. 1–2). You can access the thinking routine at https://pz.harvard.edu/sites/default/files/Take%20a%20Stand.pdf

2. Invite students to watch and/or listen to Dr. Joy Buolamwini's 2023 TED talk, "How to Protect Your Rights in the Age of AI," and discuss their reflections, questions, and opinions. Ask your students to create an educational resource in a format of their choosing—a poster, infographic, slide deck, podcast, flyer—capturing their main takeaways to share with younger students in your school district. Identify a large

language model, like ChatGPT, and large multimodal model, like an image generator, and require them to use the tools at least twice in the creation of their resource and to share a paragraph reflecting on their usage (e.g., what tools they used, whether they found them helpful [why/why not], how they prompted them, in what ways the AI supplemented rather than stood in for their own original thinking). You might even host a gallery walk, pairing students' reflections with their resources and inviting younger students, administrators, colleagues, or family members to engage with your students to become more technologically (and critically!) literate. You can access Dr. Buolamwini's TED talk at www.ted.com/talks/joy_buolamwini_how_to_protect_your_rights_in_the_age_of_ai?delay=30s&subtitle=en

References

Akselrod, O. (2023, July 3). How artificial intelligence can deepen racial and economic inequities. *American Civil Liberties Union*. www.aclu.org/news/privacy-technology/how-artificial-intelligence-can-deepen-racial-and-economic-inequities

Amazon Web Services. (2024). *What is deep learning?—Deep learning explained*. https://aws.amazon.com/what-is/deep-learning/

Ananya. (2024, March 19). AI image generators often give racist and sexist results: Can they be fixed? *Nature News*. www.nature.com/articles/d41586-024-00674-9

Bjork, C. (2023, February 9). ChatGPT threatens language diversity. More needs to be done to protect our differences in the age of AI. *The Conversation*. https://theconversation.com/chatgpt-threatens-language-diversity-more-needs-to-be-done-to-protect-our-differences-in-the-age-of-ai-198878

Brooks, T., Princess, G., Heatley, J., Kim, S., Samantha, M., Parks, S., Reardon, M., Rohrbacher, H., Sahin, B., Shani, S., James, S., Oliver, T., & Richard, V. (n.d.). Increasing threat of deepfake identities.

www.dhs.gov/sites/default/files/publications/increasing_threats_of_deepfake_identities_0.pdf

Buolamwini, J. (2018, December 18). AI, ain't I a woman? *YouTube*. www.youtube.com/watch?v=FejjAbwUqbA

Buolamwini, J. (2023a). *Unmasking AI: My mission to protect what is human in a world of machines*. Random House.

Buolamwini, J. (2023b, October). How to protect your rights in the age of AI. *TED Talk*. www.ted.com/talks/joy_buolamwini_how_to_protect_your_rights_in_the_age_of_ai?delay=30s&subtitle=en

CAST. (2024, May 14). The UDL guidelines. https://udlguidelines.cast.org/

Choi, L., & Handjojo, C. (2023, September 26). Artificial intelligence is already here. We need to make access more equitable. *EdSource*. https://edsource.org/2023/artificial-intelligence-is-already-here-we-need-to-make-access-more-equitable/697787

Collins, B. (2024, June 18). What is AI, really? An overview of AI for writers, students, and teachers. *Write the World Blog*. https://blog.writetheworld.org/what-is-ai

Greene-Santos, A. (2024). Does AI have a bias problem? *NEA*. www.nea.org/nea-today/all-news-articles/does-ai-have-bias-problem

Guinness, H. (2024, May 22). What is multimodal AI? Large multimodal models, explained. *Zapier*. https://zapier.com/blog/multimodal-ai/

Heaven, W. D. (2024, April 23). Large language models can do jaw-dropping things. But nobody knows exactly why. *MIT Technology Review*. www.technologyreview.com/2024/03/04/1089403/large-language-models-amazing-but-nobody-knows-why/?utm_source=pocket-newtab-en-us&fbclid=IwAR2Pr1EWuckq8ddPG6BVKA8RfdQrWf9tIGvB-IEwTDYOzn0hVLFvPeXOmbI

IBM. (2023, September 1). *What are AI hallucinations*? www.ibm.com/topics/ai-hallucinations

IBM Data & AI Team. (2024, April 15). AI vs. machine learning vs. deep learning vs. neural networks: What's the difference? *IBM*. www.ibm.com/think/topics/ai-vs-machine-learning-vs-deep-learning-vs-neural-networks

Merod, A. (2024, April 24). Just 18% of teachers report using AI in the classroom. *K-12 Dive*. www.k12dive.com/news/teacher-ai-use-schools/714073/

Metz, C. (2023, November 6). Chatbots may "hallucinate" more often than many realize. *The New York Times*. www.nytimes.com/2023/11/06/technology/chatbots-hallucination-rates.html

Oh, S. (2024). Carry or clutch: What about both? *Write the World Review*, 6(1), 12–14.

Project Zero, & Common Sense Media. (2021). Take a stand. *Project Zero*. https://pz.harvard.edu/resources/take-a-stand

Sahu, R. (2024, May 19). Large medical model (LMM) vs large language model (LLM). *GenHealth.ai Blog*. https://genhealth.ai/blog/large-medical-model-lmm-large-language-model-llm

Singer, N. (2023, August 24). Despite cheating fears, schools repeal ChatGPT bans. *The New York Times*. www.nytimes.com/2023/08/24/business/schools-chatgpt-chatbot-bans.html

Singer, N. (2024, April 8). Teen girls confront an epidemic of deepfake nudes in schools. *The New York Times*. www.nytimes.com/2024/04/08/technology/deepfake-ai-nudes-westfield-high-school.html

Uribe, E. S. (2024, May 14). AI boom poses threat to trans community, experts warn. *New York City News Service*. www.nycitynewsservice.com/2024/04/09/ai-threat-transgender-nonbinary-people/

West, D. M. (2024, November 20). AI poses disproportionate risks to women. *Brookings*. www.brookings.edu/articles/ai-poses-disproportionate-risks-to-women/

Poetic Reflection

Hang Onto It

Jordan Stempleman

It's useful when friendship drenched beautiful
steamrolls into all other living weight.
It's useful to say no wonder every substance is waiting
to finally mean lifetimes gone for lifetimes yet.
It's useful to begin with a near dry memory
since we're crazy for you and we refer to you so often.
It's useful to instead say air eaten mind eaten.
It's useful to see this as the companion
of all of nature to perhaps this is not our nature
to who cares and then back.
It's useful when there's this unevenly somebody else
who blurs our voice with theirs.
It's useful to shout at the park at the end of the street
please forgive me for calling this a vacation.
It's useful to write poetry when nobody's looking.
It's useful to prefer late and open with the lights on
until everything darkens into standstill and calm.

2

Applying AI to Human-Centered Pedagogy

Part I: Culturally Responsive Teaching

Marlee S. Bunch

The Heart of the Classroom

Many years ago, I had a student who, like many of us, had fear about presenting in front of the class. Beyond just being worried about presenting, she also had learning challenges, which made presenting especially daunting. Many times, she would begin speaking, then stop and ask me to just give her a zero so she did not have to present. The students in that class had become quite close, and we had a classroom culture that was supportive and understanding. Other students started to verbally encourage her, and one asked what they could do to help her. She said, "Can you all turn around so that you aren't staring at me?" Immediately, and without hesitation, all of my students turned their desks to face away from her. This show of support and gesture of understanding encouraged her, and she began the presentation again, this time completing it successfully. All of the students stood up and turned to face her, giving her a standing ovation of cheers and clapping. It was one of the most human and empathetic moments I had ever witnessed and one I will never forget. The lesson I learned in this moment was that building culturally responsive classrooms requires a foundation of respect, support, and relationship-building. This is human-centered, this is culturally responsive, and this is tending to the social and emotional needs of students and classrooms. I wonder how AI might have assisted her presentation if it had existed then. Perhaps she could have used it to practice, record her voice, and pair it with an animated version of herself, or I could have used AI to generate some techniques to help her remain calm and more at ease. Pairing AI tools with this human-centered moment that many students (and adults) struggle with would have been a worthwhile endeavor. Ultimately, elements such as these are all at the center and heart of the classroom and foundational to continuing community-immersive spaces that are human-centered.

What Are Human-Centered Pedagogy and Culturally Responsive Teaching?

One of the most important things in a classroom is when we bear witness to our students experiencing moments of genuine inquiry and excitement about learning. I recently read an essay where the author shared: "We should reject the idea that autonomous machines can exceed or replace any meaningful notion of human intelligence, creativity, and responsibility" (Shneiderman, 2021, p. 59). This quote is accurate when we think about watching a student accomplish a learning goal, smiling broadly when they receive positive feedback, or sharing their learning with fellow classmates. Moments such as these allow us to remember the power of human connection and learning present in our classrooms, especially when we stay committed to the development of the whole child. Human-centered pedagogy and teaching are rooted in what most good teachers already do—focus on students and a classroom culture that cultivates qualities such as empathy, kindness, caring, curiosity, and valuing people as individuals. These qualities are necessary to help shape students and allow for relationships to be established with students and families. Human-centered approaches might look like lessons that consider how academics can help foster individual and group qualities we hope to see, or it might look like small-group work that uses discussion to allow students to make connections with content and one another. Other approaches include celebrating cultures, using stories in our classrooms, and linking learning to things that matter to our students and communities. Additionally, human-centered pedagogy encourages educators to view their role as more than just a teacher. Human-centered teaching involves mentoring; being a role model, coach, guide, facilitator; and so on. It is what I like to call a *lighthouse teacher*. Being a *lighthouse teacher* has always reminded me of how a lighthouse stands in the distance, to help ships find their way, avoid danger, and ultimately reach their destinations or homes. Lighthouse teachers are guides and collaborators—we are not the sole keepers of knowledge, nor are we lecturing from bell to bell. Instead, we are working alongside students in tandem, there when students need guidance or knowledge, shining a light as needed to show the way and igniting or encouraging a student's own curiosity.

Today, there is no shortage of important research and relevant information about culturally responsive teaching. From Gloria Ladson-Billings to Geneva Gay, my own research, and that of many others—authors and educators have offered an abundance of information about the benefits and importance of culturally responsive teaching. This teaching has many iterations and extensions of what it encompasses as it continuously evolves and changes. At its core, culturally responsive teaching is simply good teaching. It acknowledges that our students are diverse and that this diversity requires us as educators to be informed and knowledgeable about different cultures, ethnicities, lived experiences, and communities (Ladson-Billings, 2014, 2022). Culturally responsive teaching invites us to take our students' experiences, identities, and cultures into consideration as we create and implement teaching content so that all students see themselves represented in classrooms, texts, and activities. It is the merging of practice and curricula to create an environment that builds inclusive thinking and invites us to ask, "Who is not represented here?" and "How can we expand instruction to consider students' needs?" Teachers who practice culturally responsive teaching do more than simply build tolerance for other people and perspectives—instead, they foster celebration, acceptance, understanding, and open-mindedness. I would assert that culturally responsive teaching needs one more step to help us understand its full breadth, and it is what I have termed culturally and community-immersive pedagogy. Immersion in something means being fully engaged—wholly committed, consistently practicing, and actively applying what we are learning. In that spirit, to be culturally responsive, we must be fully immersed: engaged in ongoing learning, personal growth, and willing to be in community with others as we navigate that journey. Immersion reminds us that culturally responsive teaching must be sustained, is essential for all students, and is not a passing trend we can treat as a simple box to check. In short, culturally responsive teaching is the secret sauce that helps cultivate classrooms that make everyone feel valued and welcomed, helping all students reach their highest potential (Bunch, 2024). My former student said it best when she described culturally responsive classrooms as spaces that hold up mirrors, allowing us to see the very best in ourselves and others.

How Do Culturally Responsive Classrooms Support Using AI?

Culturally responsive classrooms and AI do not seemingly go hand in hand—at least not initially. However, building culturally responsive classrooms helps to maintain the very aspects of classrooms that we are afraid AI might compromise. One of the many benefits of culturally responsive teaching and learning is that it helps to establish spaces that have clear guidelines and expectations related to how we will interact with one another and the material we encounter. Now that we have a basic understanding of what culturally responsive teaching entails, let us pause for a moment and review what culturally responsive teaching and practice are **not**:

1. Celebrating cultural holidays in isolation (e.g., calendar celebrations). A good rule of thumb is to avoid merely focusing on calendar days, food, or festivals. Culturally responsive teaching is not only about race or culture.
2. Singling out students by their identifiers or asking them to speak on behalf of their identity groups. Remember, people from shared groups are not a monolith and self-disclosure should always be up to students themselves.
3. Merely adding a few components to the curriculum (e.g., adding diverse books to a lesson or unit). It involves the culmination of practice, pedagogy, and curriculum, together with an ongoing commitment to learning.
4. Only for white teachers and/or marginalized students—rather, it is about acknowledging that the more we **all** learn and connect with others, the better our classrooms and world can become. All of us have something to learn about histories, cultures, languages, stories, systemic inequities, etc.
5. Lowering expectations. Maintaining rigorous and individualized learning for all students is essential (Hammond & Jackson, 2015).

A comprehensive understanding of culturally responsive practices will help you begin navigating and incorporating AI. Clear guidelines help classrooms navigate AI use in responsible ways that support culturally responsive principles. Together, AI can bolster our efforts to sustain culturally responsive learning, and cultural responsiveness can help us better understand and assess best uses of AI when it comes to student learning. For example, when we think about the various languages, cultures, ethnicities, levels of learning readiness, and other needs of our students, AI opens a new world of tools that can help us address these vast and varying facets. Leveraging the cultural capital that our students have (e.g., aspirational, linguistic, social, familial) can help us discover new ways to approach student learning and access the knowledge our students already possess (Yosso, 2005).

So, what are the AI tools that can elevate inclusive and equitable efforts and harness culturally responsive pedagogy? It seems that many exist, and more will quickly emerge on the scene. One of the empowering aspects of this new journey is that using these tools in a culturally responsive manner and pairing them with culturally responsive teaching practices have less to do with the tool(s) and more to do with us as the users. Therefore, **how** we interact with the tools and what red flags we look for as we are interfacing with them are key. Taking existing practices that are culturally responsive and applying them to how your students use AI tools will be a logical first step in ensuring that AI and your classroom are culturally competent.

AI in Culturally Responsive Classrooms: Potential Pitfalls

One peril of AI is that it undoubtedly lacks cultural responsiveness. We can't blame AI because, after all, it is only as culturally competent as we, collectively, are—large language models are trained on massive sets of data, and often that means content on the Internet, which contains biases reflective of those our society holds; research also tells us that the world of AI programmers lacks diversity with regard to ethnicity and gender (Picchi, 2019). "To date, the diversity problems of the AI industry and the issues of bias in the systems it builds have tended to be considered separately," authors Sarah Myers West, Meredith Whittaker, and Kate Crawford wrote. "But we suggest that these are two versions of the same problem: issues of discrimination in the workforce and in system building are deeply intertwined" (as cited in Picchi, 2019). These dual inequities—both in the AI industry and in the online data AI tools are trained on—can result in a lack of representation in what AI produces. Thus, AI can often demonstrate and/or reinforce bias, overlooking historically marginalized people and communities (e.g., this might include a preference toward images of dominant culture and Eurocentric attributes). Researchers recently shared that AI might not only discriminate but that its biases "[work] to the advantage of others, reinforcing a narrow idea of the 'normal' person" (Picchi, 2019). Bias can occur in AI tools and systems when things such as images, data, and so forth do not accurately reflect our increasingly diverse world. This bias is concerning for many reasons but, mainly, because it has the potential to reinforce stereotypes, erroneous information, and prejudice, compounding what marginalized groups already face.

Planning Curricula

The other reality that AI poses is offering ways to help teachers reduce planning time. While this is ultimately a good thing, it also creates the peril of falling into traps for quick planning. Sites such as MagicSchool offer enticing ways to save time, reduce our workload, and differentiate instruction. The site boasts that it "helps educators save time," as it offers quick lessons, assignments, assessments, project-based learning, and much more. In minutes, this site will allow you to type in a topic and return a quickly generated product—ready to print and use. This tool is similar to sites that we are currently familiar with such as Teachers Pay Teachers. The concern with sites and tools that offer access to quick lessons or content not created and vetted by the teacher using them is that they can be riddled with misinformation and lack tenets of culturally responsive teaching. For example, I recently assessed a lesson on Teachers Pay Teachers about Japanese-American incarceration camps during World War II. The lesson presented the perspective that the camps had beneficial aspects, perpetuating the idea of Asian Americans as perpetual foreigners or non-American. Even the images in the lesson reinforced falsehoods, as a picture showed young children "happily" playing outside. This lesson greatly diminished a moment in history that caused harm and trauma to humans because of racism and is an example of the dangers of using the convenience of fast lessons and the damage they can cause to our students. Therefore, teaching content produced by a tool like MagicSchool requires assessment and critical analysis to make certain that it aligns with culturally responsive practices. Consider using the Online Lesson Checklist as a way to determine if a lesson has culturally responsive principles (see Figure 2.1).

ONLINE LESSON CHECKLIST ©

You can use this checklist to assess existing lessons, evaluate online lessons, or review AI-generated lessons for culturally responsive content.

PRESENTATION OF LESSON	
The lesson clearly states the learning goal and purpose.	
It illustrates knowledge of topic, author's expertise, and includes references.	
It is free from major errors (e.g., spelling).	
It avoids using images or graphics that are stereotypical (e.g., clip art).	
It avoids relying on the 5 Fs (food, flags, festivals, famous people, and fashion).	
It offers reflection questions and opportunities to unlearn/relearn.	
It establishes early on that people can and will evolve.	
CONTENT OF LESSON	
Lesson offers context (e.g., historical) that deepens surface-level or typical knowledge.	
It highlights full breadth and complexity of individuals, communities, and cultures.	
It avoids framing people or groups solely as tragic figures.	
It avoids portraying people or groups as monoliths, tropes, or exceptions.	
It cites accurate, well-researched, and current information.	
Identify aspects of the lesson that may be problematic or require revision.	
How could the un/HUSH framework help guide any reflection or revision that is needed?	
HISTORIES AND STORIES	
The lesson includes histories and stories that are inclusive and representative.	
It uses asset-based language that affirms the strengths and identities of individuals.	
It avoids presenting limited, narrow, or stereotypical views of people.	
It celebrates and respects marginalized histories and stories.	
It acknowledges the complexity of history and does not minimize historical realities.	
It connects past to present, situating information within a broader historical context.	
Stories are multifaceted, humanizing, and reflective of lived experiences.	

FIGURE 2.1 Online Lesson Checklist

I like to think of AI as a Wikipedia of sorts—you never know what you will get, so you have to assume that the information might be unreliable. In other words, you verify, research, and check for misinformation. As educators, we often need or want to save time, and AI can certainly help, but allowing extra time to verify and assess the content AI generates is imperative. While many educator AI sites are impressive and have the potential to save time and energy, this is precisely the situation where teachers must be aware of content that might lack culturally responsive principles. Let's consider some of the elements of this AI tool: The MagicSchool site features a chatbot named Raina, which is described as an AI chatbot instructional coach. When I asked her how to create a culturally responsive classroom, within a few seconds, Raina generated this response:

To create a culturally responsive classroom, educators should consider the following strategies:

1. ***Building Relationships:*** *Get to know your students on a personal level, understand their backgrounds, and show genuine interest in their culture and experiences.*
2. ***Incorporating Diverse Perspectives:*** *Use diverse materials, literature, and resources that represent a variety of cultures, races, and backgrounds in your curriculum.*
3. ***Creating Inclusive Environment:*** *Foster a safe and welcoming space where all students feel valued and respected for who they are.*

4. ***Adapting Teaching Strategies:*** *Modify your teaching methods to accommodate different learning styles and cultural norms present in your classroom.*
5. ***Encouraging Dialogue:*** *Promote discussions about diversity, equity, and inclusion to help students understand and appreciate different perspectives.*
6. ***Professional Development:*** *Engage in continuous learning and reflection on cultural competence to enhance your teaching practices. Remember, creating a culturally responsive classroom is an ongoing process that requires dedication and an open mind to ensure all students feel seen, heard, and supported.*

(OpenAI, 2024)

This response is helpful and, in some ways, impressive, and again, the options for what the site can create and assist with are extensive. However, the problem with sites such as these is that there is enough responsiveness and impressive content that educators might be led to believe that most of the generated responses are always this reliable. It is important to keep in mind that generated lessons and activities do not naturally embed culturally responsive pedagogy, which means teachers must check each output the site generates to ensure that the content is accurate and that considerations of culturally responsive teaching are threaded throughout. Keep in mind that asking specific questions and assessing the information provided are always key when using AI platforms (Anderson, 2023). Navigating these AI spaces is where teachers will need to be acutely aware and intentional to ensure that curricula and student learning are not compromised. Countering these realities with culturally responsive practices is one important step toward reducing the risks of AI and being intentional in how we use good curricula that can be enhanced or differentiated with AI tools. Considering the benefits and perils of each tool is a great first step toward finding what works well with your classroom and what does not. The following chart offers some considerations regarding the pros/cons of various AI tools and/or platforms (see Table 2.1).

TABLE 2.1 Some Pros/Cons of AI Tools and Platforms

Considerations	Text-Generator (e.g., ChatGPT)	Collateral Generator (e.g., Magic Classroom)	Personae (e.g., Character.ai, ACTS [AI-Based Classroom Teaching Simulator])
Pros	Offers quick resolutions to questions, prompts, etc. Can provide more in-depth guidance than a general search engine, making research more efficient and specific. Can provide feedback on writing; grammar, usage, and mechanics checks may prove useful for English language learners (ELLs) and/or those with language-based learning differences.	Offers an abundance of resources and generates lessons, assessments, and a plethora of other content in minutes. Allows for quick individualization of content (such as alignment with student interests). Can supplement teachers' gaps in knowledge, offering a starting place on topics outside of teachers' areas of expertise.	Allows current and new teachers the chance to interact with AI student teachers to practice different lessons, teaching strategies, etc. This is beneficial as it allows the educator to practice without feeling judged or formally assessed. Enables students to engage in simulation activities, such as mock interviews, Socratic discussions with tutors, or chats with authors or professionals in a particular field.
Cons	Not always reliable. Can contain statements that are broad, vague, or misinformation. May have biases. Can hallucinate. Can produce content with harmful biases/stereotypes.	Can contain very generalized information, lacks details and specifics, sometimes overlooks necessary context and background information. Can hallucinate. Can produce content with harmful biases/stereotypes.	Does not offer the benefit of having a human response and/or feedback. Simulations do not account for the realities of real classrooms that navigate disruptions, students' interactions, etc. The simulations students engage in may not be culturally responsive or historically or contextually accurate/representative. Can produce content with harmful biases/stereotypes.

Another initial step as you begin this journey of using AI in your classroom will be to consider how you envision it being used. How will students use it? How will you use it (e.g., in your lessons, planning)? Finally, what roadmap will you provide students as you work with them to understand all of this new information? See Figure 2.2 for an initial checklist to consider as you begin to think through how AI will be approached and utilized in your classroom.

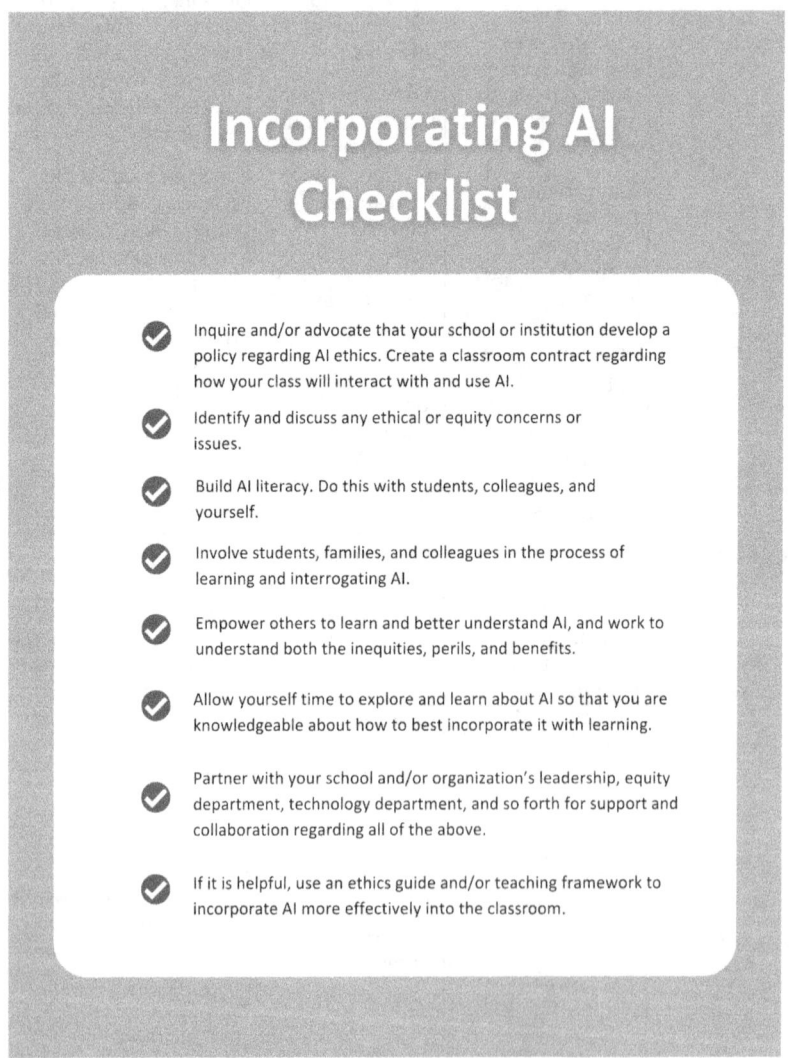

FIGURE 2.2 Incorporating AI Into Classrooms Checklist

Lessons That Keep Culturally Responsive Pedagogy Centered

My own experiences teaching have led to many lessons and areas of growth as I have moved through my career. These many years of teaching and the findings from my research led me to create a framework that would serve as a North Star for creating new lessons and/or assessing existing lessons. The un/HUSH framework is based on five guiding principles that are foundational to culturally responsive curriculum and classrooms. Using a framework such as this, or any others that encourage aspects of cultural responsiveness, is a simple way to create guardrails for keeping AI tools and usage aligned with practices that illuminate and celebrate the cultures and backgrounds of our students and global learning.

The un/HUSH framework encourages us to use the following principles when creating or assessing curricula:

1. (un) uniting for collective effort and naming our positionality—these two aspects are practices that ask us to collaborate with an awareness of each other's identities and backgrounds.
2. (H) histories—includes illuminating histories in our classrooms.
3. (U) unlearning—asks us as educators to self-reflect and fill in gaps regarding our own knowledge and learning so as to become better at our craft.
4. (S) stories—reminds us to incorporate narratives, oral histories, lived experiences, and our students' voices into the classroom to build connections and depth.
5. (H) healing—encourages dialogue and opportunities to connect to move toward collective and individual healing.

These principles help to build culturally responsive spaces and pedagogies. Additional information appears throughout this chapter to assist your use of the framework.

Before connecting AI to classroom practices, let's establish an initial foundation for how to embed culturally responsive teaching into lessons and activities, as this will be a tool to help guide us as we integrate AI into our classrooms. One of the first aspects of culturally responsive teaching involves consistent practices and mindfulness regarding how we can implement and sustain culturally responsive pedagogy. Let's begin this chapter with a brief overview of the un/HUSH framework, which offers a blueprint for culturally responsive pedagogy and learning spaces (Bunch, 2024). See Figure 2.3 for a visual snapshot of the framework and a refresher about what each principle entails.

How Can I Pair the un/HUSH Framework With AI?

Because the framework centers on collaboration, stories, dialogue, and other human-centered actions, it is an ideal tool to pair with AI, as it counterbalances technology with the elements of head and heart that we know students need. Following is an example of how you might pair the framework with AI to offer this both/and in student learning. Keep in mind that the blending of best practices, both pedagogical and technological, typically tends to serve our students and classrooms well because it gives us access to new and possible creative approaches to learning, it expands our own abilities and comfort levels with trying new things, and it offers a way to build connections and classroom culture by taking the

THE PRINCIPLES OF THE un/HUSH FRAMEWORK©

UN	H	U	S	H
Uniting for collective effort through collaborative actions. Naming our positionality to become more aware of our areas for growth.	All histories are valuable and worth being illuminated. Unearthed and unheard stories are shared.	Willingness to unlearn practices or thinking (as educators) that does not equitably serve students through reflection and self-evaluation.	Stories are bridges to understanding and connecting with others. Stories are celebrated and shared to enhance learning.	Fostering healing through positive relationships, connections, and bearing witness to one another's lives.

FIGURE 2.3 The Principles of the un/HUSH Framework

time to learn and explore unknowns collectively. In Table 2.2, you will find some specific suggestions for how the framework pairs well with AI. Keep in mind that this list will grow and change as you add your own suggestions and your students' input to these examples. Having a dedicated place where you record these additions or examples is important so that you can track your assessment and use of AI tools, how they paired well with other tools, and so forth. You might even dedicate wall space in your classroom to track this information with your students throughout the year.

TABLE 2.2 Pairing AI With un/HUSH Framework Principles

un/HUSH Framework Principle	Suggestions for Pairing With AI
(H) Histories—this principle is useful in helping discover and celebrate histories often untold or underrepresented.	Use an AI summary of a historical time period and pair it with an oral history. This is a great opportunity that allows students to verify what AI produces and build upon the historical information through research and inquiry.
(U) Unlearning—this principle is a useful tool to use self-reflection and questioning as a means to evaluate AI's responses/answers.	Before and after you or your students interact with AI, take a moment to reflect on what bias and/or misinformation might be present. What needs to be unlearned or relearned?
(S) Stories—this principle is a tool to help center stories, lived experiences, and voices.	AI is not human, so it does not have the ability to share lived experiences. This is an area where classrooms, students, and teachers will always surpass technology. One way to use AI regarding stories is to allow it to translate for our ELLs.
(H) Healing—this principle is a tool to foster healing and relationships, while encouraging connection and dialogue.	Use ChatGPT to help generate ideas for restorative justice practices; reflection prompts for journaling; discussion questions; lesson plan ideas that incorporate social-emotional learning and/or trauma-informed practices; and responses for how to consider approaching a concern that might arise in the classroom.

Now that we have reviewed the principles of the framework, let's further consider how to pair it with AI tools and how it can benefit your planning of culturally responsive teaching and the integration of AI. The un/HUSH framework is a guide to help plan culturally responsive and community-immersive lessons and activities and work toward building a classroom culture of acceptance and celebration that sustains students' love of learning and appreciation for one another. Think of the framework as a human tool to counter AI tools and one that ideally provides balance and a natural way to incorporate and sustain culturally responsive pedagogy. Having a framework paired with your pedagogy can serve as a guide and reminder for actionable ways to implement culturally responsive pedagogy.

The unlearning principle of the un/HUSH framework is a unique and important aspect that prompts us as educators to pause, reflect, and examine—again, keeping human-centered activities at the forefront. This act of reflection, especially considering the perils of AI, is imperative, as it helps us to use due diligence and take extra steps to ensure that we are pairing and integrating AI in a manner that supports cultural responsiveness and leverages equity. It also helps us to check for biases that AI might present. See Figure 2.4, which uses the principles of the framework to help you self-assess and reflect about ways that you are integrating AI in a culturally responsive manner, in addition to creating culturally responsive lessons. As you question, learn, experiment, and so forth, think of self-reflection and self-assessments as another tool that guides how AI will be used in your classroom. You could create similar self-assessment reflection questions for students to use, and this would offer another way to not only assess if AI is being used in effective ways but also open up the opportunity to check in with students about any modifications or pivoting that might need to occur. Keep in mind that students might be at varying degrees of readiness to interact with and utilize AI tools, so consistent check-ins and open communication throughout help ensure that students are getting what they need and using AI in a manner that best serves their learning.

Self-Reflection Questions: Culturally Responsive Implementation

[H] HISTORIES

How do you ensure that your lessons represent history in an accurate and inclusive manner?

Have you considered how your own positionality (lens) impacts lessons and/or AI tools?

How will you help illuminate the histories that AI might overlook?

How can you use AI to help make history relevant and connect it to the current day?

What AI tools are worth exploring when teaching history?

[U] UNLEARNING

What might AI challenge you and/or students to learn/unlearn?

What aspects of your pedagogy might need revision when integrating AI tools?

How might you use questions and reflection to unlearn/relearn?

What resources or research might support unlearning/relearning?

What culture/community/etc. would you like to learn more about to help dismantle stereotypes or racism?

[S] STORIES

How can you use stories in the classroom to stay grounded in human-centered teaching and learning?

Which stories might AI overlook or misrepresent, and how can you help ensure students are not impacted by such gaps?

How can you incorporate dialogue, writing, storytelling, and students' experiences with AI tools?

How can stories help create connection to academic content? Global and societal awareness? Real-world learning?

[H] HEALING

What AI tools might help foster healing and connection? Find two that you are willing to try.

How do your lessons leave space for dialogue and building relationships?

How might you pair AI tools with social-emotional learning or trauma-informed practices to meet the needs of all students?

Who can you partner with in your building or district to bolster practices and pedagogy centered on healing (e.g., counselors, librarians, community members)?

[UN] Uniting for collective effort and naming our positionality should always be considered. How can self-reflection and collaboration improve outcomes and experiences for all students?

FIGURE 2.4 Self-Reflection and Assessing Cultural Responsiveness

> **Box 2.1 💡 Stop and Think**

What do you already know about culturally responsive teaching, and how can this knowledge help you utilize AI to bolster culturally responsive pedagogy and principles? What questions do you have about pairing AI with culturally responsive teaching? What do you view as the potential perils of AI tools with regard to the perpetuation of biases and/or inequities? How can you counter these perils and concerns?

AI Tools

There is already a plethora of AI tools, and these will continue to grow and expand as AI evolves. Many of the tools, at first glance, are not necessarily aligned with culturally responsive teaching and learning. As discussed in previous chapters, systemic inequities and a myriad of other issues have compounded the various reasons why AI has some pitfalls regarding equity and diversity. However, your expertise and knowledge of teaching can help you to take these tools, assess their potentials and perils, and then adapt them for classroom use. Again, consider pairing AI with other culturally responsive teaching tools and, of course, with human connection and interaction. If an AI tool offers students the potential to start where they are, analyze, and consider their own lives and experiences, then it is a good start as you foster culturally responsive classrooms. If using AI allows students to discuss, build relationships, and hear the perspectives of their fellow classmates, then that is even better. Next are a few examples of how you might introduce students to using AI tools:

- ♦ Students can use AI to provide feedback on vocabulary, grammar, and mechanics. This helps students focus on their ideas and the content of their writing and alleviates some of the pressure of putting the comma in the correct place.

Follow up with students to walk through the suggestions or have them pair with a peer for review. Students can compare their original writing with the AI suggestions and think through what changes make the writing clearer.

- Students can use AI to brainstorm and generate ideas. Think of AI as a starting point, similar to using Google to begin the process of inquiry. Often, students struggle with their beginning ideas, so this is a tool that can help ignite their creativity, inquiry, and original thinking. Brainstorming is an important part of reflection, discussion, and the writing process, so ChatGPT could be used to partner with and support students in this area.
- Students can use AI to get feedback on writing or essays. I tested this use case by pasting an essay into ChatGPT and asking for feedback. The more specific my questions, the better the AI feedback. Use this as a tool in addition to peer reviews, writing workshops, and teacher feedback. Have AI offer feedback, then have students get peer feedback. They can then compare/contrast/analyze the helpfulness of each.
- Students can use AI to enhance debates, discussions, or Socratic seminars. It can help students think critically about a topic, consider counterarguments, and evaluate different elements of an argument.
- Students can use ChatGPT to begin finding resources about a topic they need to research or learn more about. It is also a good way to teach students to validate sources, consider what credible sources are, and evaluate the merits of primary versus secondary sources. Students can ask ChatGPT to find articles according to subject, grade level, reading level, language, and so forth, which individualizes the articles based on the student's specific needs and requests. Importantly, ChatGPT can sometimes hallucinate and name articles that don't actually exist, so students will need to verify any sources named in AI responses.

- Students can use ChapGPT to prepare for presentations, speeches, challenging conversations, or interviews, generating scripts or engaging in simulations as practice (we'll say more about this in chapters to come). This may help reduce worry or nerves about class presentations because it allows students to practice the skills needed to present prior to the actual activity with an audience. This is also a good tool for ELLs (English language learners).
- Students can use ChapGPT as a tool to generate journaling or writing prompts, especially those that connect curricula to students' individual lives, interests, dream careers, etc.

You will know if an AI tool is effective for student learning in many of the same ways that you assess whether or not your lessons are impactful. Consider whether students are engaged, if the lesson and/or activity promotes discussion, and if students are able to share their perspectives and witness the perspectives of their classmates. Additionally, pairing AI with the use of histories, stories, unlearning, and fostering healing are all ways to ensure that student learning will offer the concept of "windows, mirrors, and sliding glass doors," which means that students are able to see a reflection of themselves, look into the lives and perspectives of others, and have the ability to walk into the stories of others for broader understanding and immersion (Hines & Hines, 2020; Sims Bishop, 1990). All of these things foster spaces that celebrate multiple people and cultures while building knowledge and empathy.

ChatGPT, Tell Me a Story . . .

A few years into my teaching career, I met a student named Shelly (a pseudonym). She was small in stature but larger than life in so many ways. When I first met Shelly, she was quietly defiant, rarely spoke, full of fire—and yet something was behind her eyes that helped me realize there was a deeply embedded story—one that was important and connected to the young person I saw when she refused to finish an assignment or answer a question when asked. Later in the year, I started a poetry group and asked Shelly to join. She nodded silently, asked what time and day, and walked away quickly. At the first meeting, and every meeting thereafter, she showed up. At first, she just sat silently and observed, later she asked for paper and started to write, and even later she would perform in a poetry competition and share her story with the world. She shared her story of being in foster homes, her mother's addictions, and her own quest to find a sense of home. I will never forget watching her as she spoke confidently and loudly into the microphone while the audience sat silent and stunned. That is the power of the human story.

When I consider what aspects of teaching and learning are human-centered, I immediately think of writing, reading, and art. As English teachers, we have witnessed the powers of reading important texts, students finding their voices through poetry, and the exchange of ideas that happens after examining art. Reading and writing are central to all subjects and foundational to culturally responsive teaching, as they allow students the space to reflect, engage with various perspectives, and participate in inquiry-based learning. As we consider how to incorporate AI and maintain human-centered pedagogy, it makes sense to start with some examples of using AI with literacy activities (which we'll build upon in our upcoming ELA chapter). As intuitive as AI might be, there are a few aspects that it cannot replicate: the power of hearing a human tell their story and the power that is harnessed when we grapple with deeply important and complex questions. Storytelling and questions are two spaces seemingly safe from AI, so finding ways to pair them with AI will help us utilize AI as a tool. Imagine, if AI would have been a tool I could have used for Shelly, it would have allowed her to get feedback about her writing and poetry while still maintaining her shy independence and need to slowly socially integrate with students. Pairing AI with good culturally responsive teaching practices has the potential to support and foster the needs of our students by allowing us to individualize and differentiate instruction in ways not possible before. For example, changing the language of a handout or the text of an article can now be done in seconds with AI tools. This change could greatly improve how an English language learner experiences and retains the content of a lesson. ChatGPT might produce stories, but they will never be the stories of students and how our students transform throughout the year. Leveraging AI tools to benefit student learning has the potential not only to catapult learning but also to enhance the learning experiences of students. That is the story that always matters most . . .

Why Do Stories Matter?

Stories undoubtedly matter; in fact, they matter so much that current research indicates that stories have the ability to increase literacy skills, promote healing, and help us forge connections (Dutro et al., 2019). The importance of stories is something AI is also aware of. When I asked ChatGPT, "Why are stories important?," here is the response it offered:

1. *Connection*
2. *Inspiration*
3. *Learning*
4. *Preservation of Culture*

Overall, stories are a fundamental part of human communication and culture, shaping our identities, beliefs, and understanding of the world around us.

(OpenAI, 2024)

This simple inquiry reminds us that pairing stories with tools and good pedagogy is key to maintaining human-centered spaces in classrooms. Using stories in the classroom offers potential benefits for students, some of which include the following:

- Stories help create connections and build relationships.
- Stories allow students to connect learning content to real life and/or their own lives.
- Stories allow for perspective-taking and empathy to develop, allowing students to both better understand themselves and the perspectives of others.
- Stories are natural ways to celebrate and learn about other cultures and backgrounds.
- Stories allow us opportunities to be inclusive and equitable in whom we acknowledge, discuss, and learn about.
- Stories help to build listening, communication, and reflection skills.
- Stories help students analyze, structure, and assess information.
- Recent research has shown that stories and narratives are good for the brain, and neuroscience has shown that story telling has long-term positive effects on things such as "meaning making, immersion, and social connection."

(Westover, 2024)

When I initially began asking AI questions to identify areas of strength and areas of concern and/or misinformation, I recall I asked ChapGPT to tell me an important multicultural story, and sadly, the response was not what I expected. I share this story with you to both demonstrate the importance of experimenting with tools and the areas where AI can mislead learning or misrepresent concepts related to culturally responsive teaching. The fact that, when asked about multicultural stories, AI did not generate factual information connected to humans is cause for caution and concern (Akselrod, 2023). The response, shown in Figure 2.5, offers a story about the Monkey

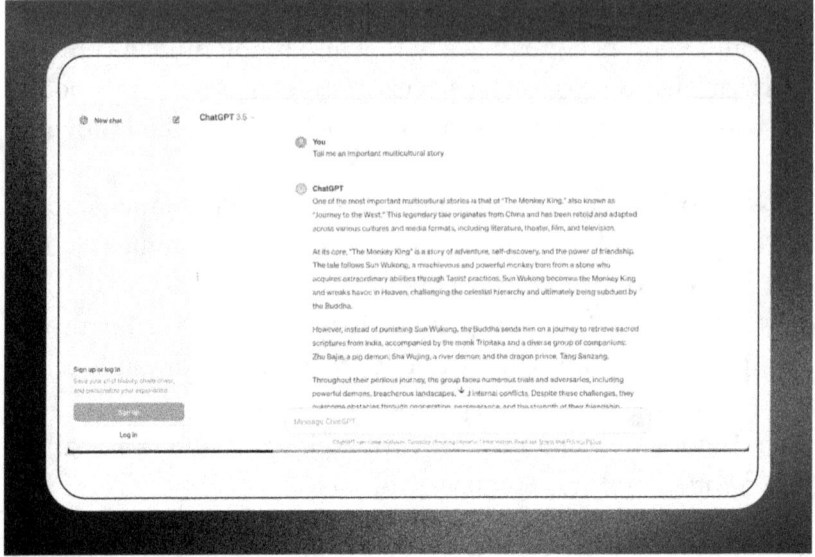

FIGURE 2.5 Sample ChatGPT Response: Multicultural Story

King, and while this might be an entertaining children's movie, fable, or fictional story, it certainly did not meet the goal of telling me a human story that illuminated or celebrated a culture and/or person. There is potential to perpetuate harmful cultural stereotypes, even in fiction, and we must be aware of this when considering books, films, and other media that our students are exposed to. It has been mentioned that the story of the Monkey King by Wu Cheng'en could be based on a historical monk from the Chinese Tang Dynasty, but even so, the response did not adequately answer the question in my prompt. What this illustrates is the manner in which AI can misread our questions or prompts and offer information unrelated to the knowledge we are trying to gain. It also illustrates that the prompt I asked was too vague. In short, the answer I received was partially due to my own error of not asking a good question. Asking rich questions, identifying misinformation, and learning to assess the information AI produces are important (OpenAI, 2024).

Revising my question to "Tell me an important, multicultural nonfiction story about justice," yielded better results.

One powerful nonfictional multicultural story that illustrates the journey towards justice is the life of Nelson Mandela, particularly focusing on his fight against apartheid in South Africa.

Nelson Mandela was a pivotal figure in the struggle against apartheid, a system of institutionalized racial segregation and discrimination enforced by the South African government from 1948 to 1994. Born in 1918, Mandela became involved in the African National Congress (ANC) in the 1940s, advocating for equal rights and the end of apartheid.

In 1964, Mandela was sentenced to life in prison for his activism and leadership against apartheid. He spent 27 years in prison, during which his cause gained international attention and support. Mandela's imprisonment became a symbol of the global struggle against racial oppression and injustice.

Throughout his imprisonment, Mandela remained steadfast in his commitment to justice and equality. He negotiated with the South African government from his prison cell, eventually leading to his release in 1990 amid growing international pressure and internal reforms within South Africa.

After his release, Mandela continued his work towards justice, leading negotiations to dismantle apartheid and establish multiracial elections in 1994. Mandela became South Africa's

> *first black president in the country's first fully representative democratic election, marking the end of apartheid and the beginning of a new era of reconciliation and nation-building.*
>
> *Mandela's story is a testament to the power of perseverance, resilience, and nonviolent resistance in the face of injustice. His leadership and dedication to equality inspired millions around the world and continue to serve as a beacon of hope and courage in the ongoing struggle for justice and human rights globally.*
>
> (OpenAI, 2024)

Let us think through the steps we had to take in order to get better results from AI:

Step 1: Ask a question with cultural responsiveness in mind. Also consider the learning objectives and how they align with what is being asked.

Step 2: Assess the results the prompt generates. Check for factual information, vagueness, missing information, and whether the response is applicable to the question that was asked.

Step 3: Consider and assess the initial question that was asked. Consider if the prompt is relevant, factual, and specific. Does it need to be revised, made more specific, etc.? If so, ask a revised question and wait for the AI response.

Step 4: Repeat Step 2 to assess new information AI generates.

Discovering ways to help AI support incorporating stories in lessons and activities is a worthwhile endeavor, though it may prove to be an area where AI could be misleading or lack accuracy (Al-Sibai, 2024). However, taking time to evaluate and work through these gray areas is important, since literacy and sharing culturally relevant stories of representation will benefit all students. Not only does incorporating stories in the classroom provide academic and social benefits for learners, but it also is a human-centered element that can help counterbalance AI. After all, stories told by humans with lived experiences will always resonate.

Thomas King captured it best when he said, "The truth about stories is that's all we are" (2011, p. 2). This quote summarizes why maintaining stories, narratives, and poetry in the classroom is paramount to students' success (both academically and socially). If Thomas King's assertion is correct, then instead of worrying about what AI might do to our classrooms, we should focus instead on what AI will do to our classrooms if stories are absent.

How can we pair AI with classroom culture and curricular content to help unearth, celebrate, and amplify stories not typically told? How can students use AI as a way to explore interests and questions that might help them make sense of their own stories? Of other people's stories? Of global stories? If stories are all we are, then AI can never do the things we fear. Flying robots, the Jetsons, and scenes from *The Mitchells vs. the Machines* become merely fictional worries if we drill down on three elements that help center stories in our classrooms: (1) sharing personal and multi-genre stories that broaden students' perspectives, (2) asking the right questions, and (3) centering conversations and dialogue.

These three elements will help you assess and ensure that lessons and activities are human-centered and rooted in culturally responsive teaching.

Returning to Narrative

When I began my teaching career, personal narratives were commonplace in the classroom and an integral part of the curriculum, as states considered narrative writing a tested skill. Students wrote memoirs and other forms of writing that allowed them to tell their stories. It was always a favorite assignment that offered students a chance to self-reflect, consider their experiences, and use writing as a means of enjoyment and catharsis. In recent years, narrative writing is more scarce in the classroom as analysis, persuasive writing, and other forms have taken precedence. However, as noted previously, narrative writing, narrative inquiry, and stories have academic and socio-emotional benefits that we cannot overlook. Clandinin and Rosiek discuss the relevance of stories:

> Human beings have lived out and told stories about that living for as long as we could talk. And then we have talked about the stories we tell for almost as long. These lived and told stories and the talk about the stories are one of the ways . . . we fill our world with meaning and enlist one another's assistance in building lives and communities.
> (Clandinin & Rosiek, 2007, p. 35)

The following quote further illustrates the power of stories when used within our curriculum:

> Imagining pedagogy through the transcendent power of story, we see how much difference, openness, and place matter. As we are quieted by these thoughts, wonders emerge. We wonder, for example, about possibilities for storying and restorying ourselves and one another into being; we wonder about new kinds of, or maybe forgotten or written over, obligations and ways of interacting and responding to and with one another.
> (Huber et al., 2013, p. 216)

Stories offer a bridge to better understanding ourselves and others. Stories and narrative writing are examples of human-centered learning that allows us to center students and relationship-building.

Brittany and I have witnessed this power firsthand, and as I think back to the writing activities that were most effective with our students, a few come to mind:

1. Ask students to select a color, or randomly assign one. Then ask students to write a short narrative about a memory that connects to the color. You can incorporate AI tools by having AI offer feedback on a draft of their

assignment or suggest obscure colors students may not be familiar with but that may spark creative writing.
2. Ask students to interview someone of their choice. You could also ask them to interview another student in the class. Then, have students write a short narrative about the person they interviewed. Again, AI can offer feedback or support learners who might need more guidance, generate interview questions, or allow students to engage in a simulated practice interview before interacting with their human subject.
3. While teaching a class at Smith College, Brittany and I asked students to gather in small groups of 3–4 students. Each student would begin by telling a story, and then pass to the next student who would continue the story. This is done out loud, allowing students to see how stories build and change. This activity continues until the teacher ends it (this can be a timed activity). You might use AI to generate prompts/topics to spark this small-group verbal activity.

Exercises like these offer quick opportunities for students to practice skill building, expand their knowledge of self and others, and become co-creators in their learning—all of which are critical skills in culturally responsive teaching. Narrative writing offers a way to blend human-centered learning with emerging AI tools. Offering students curriculum and activities that are relevant, relatable, and innovative is culturally responsive and makes learning more engaging. Table 2.3 offers some options for creating activities that pair AI tools with various ways to practice; again, we will explore even more strategies in the chapter addressing English language arts instruction. See Table 2.4 for the potential teacher benefits of AI.

TABLE 2.3 Pairing AI Tools and Practice

Activity	*Objective/Learning Skill*
Students can use AI to produce an essay and then assess what could be improved about the writing—	This allows students to practice feedback and analyze writing in an objective manner. Instead of being asked

(Continued)

TABLE 2.3 (Continued)

Activity	Objective/Learning Skill
what gaps exist. AI assists with editing a first draft before the class moves to peer editing and feedback.	to critique their peers, they can learn how to give effective feedback through a neutral mode. This helps students learn what feedback and editing can look like so more effective peer editing occurs.
Students can experiment with ChatGPT so they can use it as a learning tool—for example, asking good questions.	Practicing inquiry-based thinking and learning inspires students to ask better, more essential questions.
Teachers can use AI to help translate and bridge language gaps.	Using AI as a tool for ELLs is a wonderful way to honor students' languages while also engaging their learning needs.
Students can use AI to practice their speaking skills. This can potentially be used for practice with presenting, language acquisition, and so forth.	This helps ELL students, students who are shy, students with speech concerns, or students with social anxieties. This tool can benefit all students, as most of us benefit from individual practice.
AI tutoring can be used to help students with writing and/or reading activities.	AI has the capability to help students learn information that they need help with, offering the potential for additional support.
AI translation services and tools can support ELLs.	Allows students and educators to easily translate texts and/or speaking, giving us better access and connections to a multilingual world.
Language learning support and practice facilitated by AI can guide students as they work toward language acquisition and offer individualized instruction.	Practice with language acquisition skills.

TABLE 2.4 Potential Teacher Benefits of AI

Teacher Learning	Benefit and Skill
Use AI to create more robust discussions.	AI can help educators navigate and practice having discussions related to equity and

(Continued)

TABLE 2.4 (Continued)

Teacher Learning	Benefit and Skill
	inclusion. What we might consider difficult conversations can now be practiced with AI. The Reach Every Reader Project through Harvard, for example, uses "digital puppeteering to help teachers practice equitable discussion leading" (Dede, 2023, as cited in Anderson, 2023).
Use the un/HUSH framework to deepen the information AI generates.	Consider (un)—Uniting for collective effort and naming our positionality, (H)—Histories, (U)—Unlearning, (S)—Stories, (H)—Healing. See Figure 2.4 for additional information regarding these pedagogical elements. This will help you check for culturally responsive principles.
Use AI to help you identify your own knowledge gaps.	This will help you not only become a better user of AI, but also help you better assess existing lessons, resources, etc., that may lack cultural responsiveness.
Use AI to differentiate lessons and content for students.	This will save time and also help you to ensure that you are meeting the unique needs of your students.

Asking the Right Questions: The Art of Inquiry

Helping students develop critical inquiry skills is always a goal when teaching. We know that asking good questions helps students develop foundational learning that they will need beyond the middle and post-secondary classrooms (Lee & Kinzie, 2012). Pairing AI with an inquiry model is a good way to help students further develop these skills, along with analytical thinking. As educators, we can help guide students to develop these skills by making certain that we help them to understand how to make meaning on their own accord. "A good educator is eliciting answers from a student and they're not telling students things. I think that's a really nice distinction between co-intelligence as a thought partner and AI doing the work for you" (Klein, 2024). Teaching students to ask the right questions is undoubtedly an important skill, and recent research illustrates that inquiry-based learning proves beneficial for students and classrooms. AI will ask us to consider not only the quality of questions we ask but also the types of questions we ask, so teaching students both of these skills is important as we work toward leveraging AI as a tool (Stern et al., 2017). *The Art of Socratic Questioning* by Dr. Richard Paul and Dr. Linda Elder helps us to begin thinking through how we will help students establish a foundation for asking complex and deep questions that require analysis and critical thinking. See Figure 2.6 for a visual guide to helping students begin practicing the art of questioning.

Helping Students Ask the Right Questions

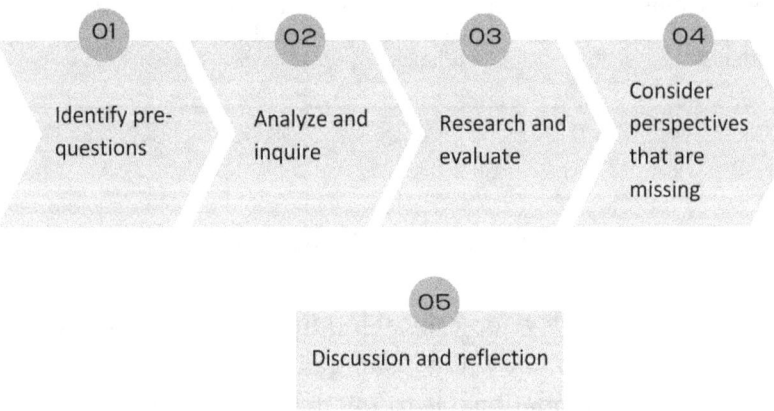

FIGURE 2.6 Helping Students Ask the Right Questions Guide

Types of Questions

There are many types of questions that we can ask, so helping students narrow their questions and practice using the correct type of questioning is important, especially when navigating AI and the content AI produces. Dr. Richard Paul and Dr. Linda Elder have researched and written about questions and critical thinking. They designed various questions central to building good thinking and analytical skills; we have adapted it as shown in Table 2.5. As AI becomes more advanced and more intuitive, even progressing beyond prompts, the skill of teaching students to ask good questions will never go out of style. Teaching students to ask questions, understand various levels of questioning, and then analyze those questions and answers are among the best ways you can prepare students to interact with AI (Lee & Kinzie, 2012).

TABLE 2.5 Types of Questions

Fact-Based Questions	*Opinion-Based Questions*	*Critical Questions*	*AI Usage Questions*
This type of question requires analysis, reasoning, and evidence. This type of question offers a specific answer. This type of question requires students to use facts and procedures to obtain the correct answer.	Opinion-based questions spark us to consider our own preferences and opinions; the answer may be subjective.	Critical questions require reasoning, inquiry, and analysis. Students have to rely on reasoning to discern the answer(s).	1. What types of questions are we asking AI? 2. How many possible answers are there? What types of answers are there (e.g., factual, conceptual, subjective)? 3. What research or sources do we need to affirm that AI is accurate? 4. How can we use what AI tells us to learn more and ask deeper questions? 5. What prior questions or information related to the topic or content already exist?

(Continued)

TABLE 2.5 (Continued)

Fact-Based Questions	Opinion-Based Questions	Critical Questions	AI Usage Questions
Examples:	Examples:	Examples:	Examples:
Who are some influential Indigenous rights activists? What coalitions have historically supported civil rights?	Should we recognize holidays in school? Should books be banned?	How can we make education more equitable? How can we reverse climate change?	After asking AI to define culture, the class might discuss: What can culture tell us about a community, time period, person?

Building time into lessons to better understand AI's limitations and benefits is important, and asking questions is a simple yet effective way to begin this process. We cannot understand something, or how to use it, until we cross the threshold of fear and begin engaging with it. What might this look like? One way to start is by encouraging students to ask questions as they assess and evaluate the information that AI generates (see Box 2.2 and Box 2.3). This process can be a collective endeavor that also builds classroom cohesion and inquiry. Another step is taking time for you (as the educator) and your students to experiment with AI and learn about it through hands-on interaction (Stern et al., 2017).

Box 2.2 Questions to Help Evaluate AI Information

- Is this information accurate? What might be inaccurate? Consider the summary/summaries offered—evaluate them.
- How do we know if this information is reliable or not? How can I fact-check this information? What information do we need or want to spend more time with?
- What accurate research can I find to validate or reinforce this information?

- What aspects of the AI response/answer are potentially made up, false, or unexpected? What biases from AI are present?
- What are we missing? What information might we be missing that prevents us from assessing whether information is valid? To whom or where can we go to get additional information and context?

To get better results from AI (Mollick & Mollick, 2024):

"Give AI a persona." For example, if you are using it to help students practice for a presentation, tell AI that it is an audience member judging a speech. "AI wants to slot into a story, so if we are not explicit, it will attempt to find a dialogue. Assigning a personality to it that will work best for your goals, prevents it from randomly choosing one."

- Asking better and more specific questions seems to generate better responses.
- Acting conversationally is the best approach.
- Giving personas and context helps generate better information.

Building critical thinking skills can help students evaluate whether or not the information they receive from AI is accurate.

Box 2.3 Questions You Can Use to Evaluate AI Answers

What accounts for _____? How did _____ occur?

Are there any reasons to doubt this answer? What might AI be implying by giving this answer, and/or what might AI be overlooking?

How could we determine if this answer is true or not? How can we discern that this conclusion is correct?

What evidence or research supports this response? How can we evaluate this information?

What other questions might we need the answer in order to have more information about this? What analysis needs to occur to figure out _____?

What objections to this answer might exist? What counter-arguments exist?

How can we check this answer for biases? Whose voices might add to this conversation?

Box 2.4 Try Out the Tech and Reflect

Take a moment to ask ChatGPT questions about culturally responsive teaching. After reviewing the answer(s) ChatGPT generates, consider any gaps or revisions that may be necessary. Finally, reflect by making a short list of your greatest concerns about AI. What resources or research might help you learn enough to alleviate some of your concerns? Consider asking it to tell you one of the following:

1. How can I build a culturally responsive classroom?
2. How can AI help me with culturally responsive teaching?
3. How can I create culturally responsive lessons and assessments?

After reviewing the answer(s) ChatGPT generates, consider any gaps or revisions that may be necessary. Finally, reflect by making a short list of your greatest concerns about AI. What resources or research might help you learn enough to alleviate some of your concerns?

References

Akselrod, O. (2023, July 3). How artificial intelligence can deepen racial and economic inequities: ACLU. *American Civil Liberties Union.* www.aclu.org/news/privacy-technology/how-artificial-intelligence-can-deepen-racial-and-economic-inequities

Al-Sibai, N. (2024, June 7). AI systems are learning to lie and deceive, scientists find. *Futurism.* https://futurism.com/ai-systems-lie-deceive

Anderson, J. (2023). Educating in a world of artificial intelligence. *Harvard Graduate School of Education.* www.gse.harvard.edu/ideas/edcast/23/02/educating-world-artificial-intelligence

Bunch, M. S. (2024). *The magnitude of us: An educator's guide to creating culturally responsive classrooms.* Teachers College Press.

Clandinin, D. J., & Rosiek, J. (2007). Mapping a landscape of narrative inquiry: Borderland spaces and tensions. In D. J. Clandinin (Ed.), *Handbook of narrative inquiry: Mapping a methodology* (pp. 35–75). Sage.

Dutro, E., Campano, G., & Ollett, M. (2019). *The vulnerable heart of literacy: Centering trauma as powerful pedagogy.* Teachers College Press.

Hammond, Z., & Jackson, Y. (2015). *Culturally responsive teaching and the brain: Promoting authentic engagement and rigor among culturally and linguistically diverse students.* Corwin, a SAGE Company.

Hines, E., & Hines, M. (2020, August 11). Want to support Black students? Invest in Black teachers. *Time.* https://time.com/5876164/black-teachers/

Huber, J., Caine, V., Huber, M., & Steeves, P. (2013). Narrative inquiry as pedagogy in education: The extraordinary potential of living, telling, retelling, and reliving stories of experience. *Review of Research in Education, 37,* 212–242. www.jstor.org/stable/24641962

King, T. (2011). *The truth about stories: A native narrative.* House of Anansi Press.

Klein, A. (2024, October 24). AI and equity, explained: A guide for K–12 schools. *Education Week.* www.edweek.org/technology/ai-and-equity-explained-a-guide-for-k-12-schools/2024/06

Ladson-Billings, G. (2014). Culturally relevant pedagogy 2.0 a.k.a. The remix. *Harvard Educational Review, 84*(1), 74–84. https://doi.org/10.17763/haer.84.1.p2rj131485484751

Ladson-Billings, G. (2022). *The dreamkeepers: Successful teachers of African American children.* John Wiley & Sons, Incorporated.

Lee, Y., & Kinzie, M. B. (2012). Teacher question and student response with regard to cognition and language use. *Instructional Science, 40*(6), 857–874. www.jstor.org/stable/43575388

Mollick, E. R., & Mollick, L. (2024). Instructors as innovators: A future-focused approach to new AI learning opportunities, with prompts. *SSRN Electronic Journal.* https://doi.org/10.2139/ssrn.4802463

OpenAI. (2024). *ChatGPT* (Jan 8 version) [Large language model]. https://chat.openai.com/chat

Paul, R., & Elder, L. (2019). *The Thinker's Guide to the art of Socratic questioning.* Foundation for Critical Thinking.

Picchi, A. (2019, April 17). How tech's white male workforce feeds bias into AI. *CBS News.* www.cbsnews.com/news/ai-bias-problem-techs-white-male-workforce/

Shneiderman, B. (2021). Human-centered AI. *Issues in Science and Technology, 37*(2), 56–61. https://www.jstor.org/stable/27092030

Sims Bishop, R. (1990). Mirrors, windows, and sliding glass doors. *Perspectives: Choosing and Using Books From the Classroom, 6*(3), ix–xi. https://scenicregional.org/wp-content/uploads/2017/08/Mirrors-Windows-and-Sliding-Glass-Doors.pdf

Stern, J., Ferraro, K., & Mohnkern, J. (2017). *Tools for teaching conceptual understanding: Designing lessons and assessments for deep learning.* Corwin.

Westover, J. H. (2024, January 11). The power of storytelling: How our brains are wired for narratives. *HCI Consulting.* www.innovativehumancapital.com/post/the-power-of-storytelling-how-our-brains-are-wired-for-narratives

Yosso, T. J. (2005). Whose culture has capital? *Race, Ethnicity and Education, 8*(1), 69–91. https://doi.org/10.1080/1361332052000341006

Poetic Reflection

Beside the Vending Machine

Jordan Stempleman

The foreign country is indeed the size of you,
Tugging at the economy of your seeing, proportions
That never breakdown into sameness until no, until yes

That at work I got in late today because it's such an old
Fashioned place, one person sleeping while
Heavy around them, the world backed down and woke up

That while you work, you are accustomed, no god
In an unmade bed who knew not how
The emptiness about things still stands

That in this place, a reserve of the explained, it all goes
Without saying, a warehouse of everywhere,
This revolved housing, a sameness if collected only as

Seemed, as sameness to loop easily the familiar,
As foreignness itself is where we began from, and
While we are here, we will speak this circulation

3

Applying AI to Human-Centered Pedagogy

Part II: Social-Emotional Learning

Brittany R. Collins

Mike (a pseudonym) was a 12-year-old humor writer and cat lover. He had his own blog, on which he posted short stories featuring felines, faraway galaxies, and a wit that seemed far beyond his age. He also had a severe neuromuscular condition that rendered him paralyzed with the exception of movement in one of his index fingers—which he used, through a special computer hookup attached to his wheelchair, to write stories for his website.

I first met Mike while teaching a virtual creative writing workshop for teens in the summer of 2022; requiring a ventilator and trach, he needed a little more time on certain assignments, and his parents sat by his side—out of the Zoom frame—to repeat his verbal contributions for the group to understand.

Mike was the most engaged, enthusiastic, and verbal participant in our group, always the first to offer a warm, eager "hello" as we settled into our sessions. Throughout our time together, Mike began to include in his stories characters who also used wheelchairs and breathing supports. But his characters' limitations were never the focus of the story—merely characterization details, like hair or eye color. His characters were heroes, conquering battles in alternate worlds.

In every class that I teach, I conclude with a "thinking routine" from Harvard Graduate School of Education's Project Zero in which students complete the sentence frame, "I used to think . . . Now I think . . ." (2015, p. 1).

When I facilitated this activity with Mike and his fellow workshop participants, he shared in the chat that he never realized he could write characters who share his identity, but he now thinks fiction can be a powerful way to do so.

I learned many lessons from Mike that summer. I learned that the colloquialism coined by children's literature researcher Rudine Sims Bishop in 1990, about stories being "windows, mirrors, and sliding glass doors" (Strobbe, 2021, p. 1), referenced previously by Marlee, is not just theoretical—that stories hold real power to reflect and affirm youths' identities. I rediscovered that educational technology can open a world otherwise closed—a truism I already knew having acquired my own physical disability as a college student, becoming reliant on virtual mediums to learn and, later, to teach in an accessible way. And I was reminded—watching Mike's peers include him in breakout room group work, cheer him on in the chat, and consider his literary contributions through peer review—that social-emotional learning (SEL) is much more than an add-on, a box to check while lesson planning; it is deeply interwoven with every facet of the learning experience, but its lessons are overt or covert, depending on how intentional we, as teachers, are in our planning.

Mike, then, became a nexus for considering the intersections of accessibility, equity, technology, and human connection. Indeed, without all of these variables, we never would have met, never would have learned with and from each other. When considering AI tools, I hold students like Mike in my mind. How can we use technology to access and engage more students than ever before? How can we use it to inspire students to be more inclusive, reflective, and connective young people? Can we leverage large language models (LLMs) to bring social-emotional learning to life? No matter how surreal it may seem, can we use something that isn't sentient to make ourselves more so?

ChatGPT made its debut while I was a graduate student studying social-emotional learning at the University of Virginia, so I felt intrigued to consider whether and how we might use it with students as a relational playground, a sandbox in which to support core social-emotional competencies, metacognition, and more. The most commonly cited definition of SEL comes from the Collaborative for Academic, Social, and Emotional Learning (CASEL), stating that it is

> the process through which all young people and adults acquire and apply the knowledge, skills, and attitudes to develop healthy identities, manage emotions and achieve personal and collective goals, feel and show empathy for others, establish and maintain supportive relationships, and make responsible and caring decisions.
>
> (CASEL, 2023)

It's not all touchy-feely—targeting these facets of youth development demonstrates widespread, concrete benefits. Researchers have long found, for example, that engagement in SEL programs results in 11 percentile point gains in students' academic achievement; the seminal meta-analytic study revealing this impact, published in 2011, has been cited over 11,000 times (Durlak et al., 2011).

And in a 2023 meta-analysis examining 424 studies from 53 countries, implicating 575,361 students in grades K–12, Cipriano et al. found that students who participated in "universal school-based social and emotional learning interventions . . . experienced significantly improved skills, attitudes, behaviors, school climate and safety, peer relationships, school functioning, and academic achievement" (2023, p. 1181).

There is a great need for accessible social-emotional learning programming that ensures all students can reap these benefits; SEL is shown to support youth mental health, with researchers at the Yale School of Medicine—including Christina Cipriano, PhD, associate professor at the Yale Child Study Center and first author of the 2023 meta-analysis mentioned above—highlighting that students who participate in SEL programs report improvements in "anxiety, stress, depression, and suicidal thoughts" (Brough, 2023). In an age when one in seven adolescents experiences a mental health disorder (World Health Organization, 2024); two-thirds of U.S. youth have experienced trauma (SAMHSA, 2024), and researchers are revealing the ways in which early life adversity can impact brain connectivity, structure, and function into adulthood (Teicher et al., 2016), such findings about the efficacy of SEL are profound, and they make the prospect of omnipresent AI tools promising if those tools can, indeed, support this type of pedagogy and allow educators to implement it responsibly and at scale.

Equally important—and evident in the CASEL definition cited before—is that SEL is not psychotherapy. Educators are not, and should not be positioned as, trained mental health interventionists. (As an aside, we note that as AI therapy tools emerge, with bots trained to respond to youth inputs using output language aligned with techniques from cognitive- and dialectical-behavior therapy among other theoretical modalities, some schools may turn to AI in an attempt to increase access to mental health support for the 653,700 U.S. youth who lack a school-based mental health professional (Solis, 2024). At the time of our writing this, we view this prospect as exceedingly fraught. Given the highly sensitive nature of mental health disclosures, and, in some cases, the need for urgent intervention best done by humans with extensive training, along with the other caring adults in students' lives, we do not recommend these AI technologies at this time.)

Though studies reveal that SEL can benefit youth mental health, SEL itself does **not**—contrary to what some popular media may suggest—involve eliciting students' personal stories or processing their adverse life experiences. Instead, SEL programming, which is rooted in the teaching of interpersonal and relational skills, fits within the curricular interventions already occurring in classrooms. Specifically, SEL presents a universally applicable approach to teaching five distinct competencies, defined by CASEL (2023) as

- Self-awareness
- Self-management
- Social awareness
- Relationship skills
- Responsible decision-making

When considering how to overlay AI, it is these competencies on which we'll focus.

Importantly, the following activities and strategies are propositions—not empirically researched teaching strategies. In this time of AI nascency, we take to this chapter the approach of using AI as a way to experiment, test, hypothesize, and try out new approaches to using technology to enhance SEL. We encourage you to revise, adapt, or edit any of the ideas you see here to make them your own for you and your students as we all learn and grow with these novel tools.

Self-Awareness

Self-awareness is, in many ways, the bedrock of all other social-emotional skills. Being able to attune to, reflect upon, analyze, and understand oneself—to engage in metacognition, or thinking about one's thinking—is at the core of all learning, whether academic or relational. But self-awareness is, perhaps paradoxically, challenging to foster in isolation; like a children's book author who needs a skilled editor to highlight a plot hole, a client who benefits from the incisive questions of a counselor, or a musical apprentice who benefits from frequent reminders about technique from a mentor, we all need to see ourselves reflected back through the eyes of another in order to achieve clarity and growth.

Organizational psychologist Tasha Eurich emphasizes this dynamic by positing that there are two types of self-awareness, both critical to success in career and life:

> Across the studies we examined, two broad categories of self-awareness kept emerging. The first, which we dubbed internal self-awareness, represents how clearly we see our own values, passions, aspirations, fit with our environment, reactions (including thoughts, feelings, behaviors, strengths, and weaknesses), and impact on others. We've found that internal self-awareness is associated with higher job and relationship satisfaction, personal and social control, and happiness; it is negatively related to anxiety, stress, and depression. The second category, external self-awareness, means understanding how other people view us, in terms of those same factors listed above.
> (2018, p. 1)

In the classroom, there are several ways we may incorporate AI to cultivate internal self-awareness in students and to supplement our serving as mirrors in their development of external self-awareness, as well. Let's consider them.

Internal Self-Awareness

Student Journaling

Perhaps the lowest hanging fruit for using AI to support students' internal self-awareness is to use it as a prompt generator for journaling provocations designed to support self-reflection; despite the basic nature of this use case, it is still significant—as 84% of the 2,531 teacher-respondents to a 2024 Pew Research Center Survey reported not having enough time to complete the administrative, curricular, and instructional components of their jobs, which greatly limits opportunities for the creation of new content, especially content that is individualized according to students' interests and needs (Lin et al., 2024; Walker, 2024). At a time when teaching is purported to be as stressful as working as an ER doctor and nearly 50% of teachers leave the profession within five years (Collins, 2024), the prospect of a virtual content-creation assistant holds weight.

So, I told ChatGPT-4o:

> You are a ninth-grade English language arts teacher who wants to support students' social-emotional learning, especially their self-awareness. Many of your students resist writing. They are passionate about sports, music, and science fiction. Create 10 journaling prompts designed to support their self-awareness skills.

In less than a minute, I had 10 feasible prompts—to build upon or edit to my liking—that I could dole out according to my knowledge of students' interests. Here are some of the most notable:

Sports and Challenges:

Describe a challenging moment you faced in a sport or physical activity. How did you feel at that moment, and how did you overcome it? What did you learn about yourself through this experience?

Music and Emotions:

Think about a song that deeply resonates with you. Write about why this song is meaningful to you and how it reflects your emotions or experiences. What does this reveal about your feelings or personal values?

Sci-Fi and Aspirations:

Imagine you are a character in a science fiction world with special abilities or futuristic technology. Write about a day in your life in that world. How do your strengths and interests shape your actions and choices in this scenario?

(OpenAI, 2024)

We might now begin class with five minutes of guided freewriting, prioritizing tenets of student-centered learning by providing customized prompts according to students' interests, without having to take time to create 10 separate prompts. Instead, we can focus on the relationship-building required to truly ascertain and appreciate students' interests, strengths, and areas for growth. Or we can hone our focus on facilitating authentic dialogue between students—for example, asking them to read or summarize their freewriting in response to these prompts and to then identify common themes across their and their peers' reflections—moving from self-awareness toward other social-emotional competencies, like social awareness and relationship skills (CASEL, 2023).

Scaffolding Verbal Processing

In my professional learning work with teachers, I often hear that with social-emotional learning (or, relatedly, trauma-informed, grief-responsive teaching), they don't know where to begin. They're committed to the ethos, they want to support students' skills, but the topic(s) feel much more amorphous than, say, teaching the Civil War. When we as instructors feel anxious or intimidated, we might also experience a stress response, which impairs our higher cognitive functions and makes it harder to think on our feet, which is a critical component of effective teaching (Schimelpfening, 2023). To avoid such a dynamic while working toward our goal of supporting SEL, it can feel helpful to have some phrases on hand—some scripts to use with students. Here, again, we might position AI as the teacher and ask it to generate some ready-made scaffolds. For example, to support my goal of scaffolding students' internal self-awareness through one-on-one conferencing, I prompted:

> You are a ninth-grade English language arts teacher who wants to build your students' self-awareness skills. One way you'll do so is through one-on-one conferencing sessions in which you workshop students' writing and course progress. What are some questions and/or phrases you can use to support students' self-awareness in these discussions?

In response, I received an almost overwhelming amount of content—questions to support students' self-awareness, goal-setting, progress tracking, and revision in connection with writing assignments; self-awareness in course progress, from general reflections and affective reactions to the course, to self-assessment and goal-setting; and phrases that I could use to support students' self-awareness and growth mindset, encourage metacognition, and cultivate emotional and social awareness.

Looking back at the prompt, I see that I included multicomponent requests connected to each of these areas—the AI generated statistically plausible additions, like metacognition—yet I can't help but feel, as the human using the tool, that the AI has somehow intuited my intent, somehow found the words I was grasping for but couldn't quite reach. This reinforces, for me, both the potential of AI—to support the harried teacher in a moment of need—and the perils, as we think about students who may blindly believe or feel a sense of relationship with these tools—a trust that may be violated or that may give way to an authority fallacy (the belief that, if someone or something in a position of power says something, it's inherently true). All of this reinforces our need to teach critical literacy.

But back to the outputs: In the scenario described, I could now walk into an individualized conferencing session ready to support students' internal self-awareness with AI-generated questions like "What strategies do you use when you're stuck on a writing task? How effective are they? How do you decide when a piece of writing is finished? When you receive feedback, how do you determine which suggestions to implement?" Or, I could check in more broadly about the course: "What are your academic goals for this semester? How do you plan to achieve them? Can you identify any specific habits that have helped you succeed?" And I could reinforce what students tell me, using sentence frames and declarative language like "I noticed that you ... (e.g., used vivid imagery, structured your argument well). How did you decide to do that?" (OpenAI, 2024).

Of course, we as educators are already extensively trained in the art of inquiry and the role of spotlight language in supporting students' thinking—but when encountering instructional topics or dynamics that feel new or opaque, we now have an added tool to ground us in that training, tailored to a specific skill (e.g., internal self-awareness). Such a tool may feel most helpful for new teachers finding their way: Ethan Mollick, professor of management at Wharton and a foremost thought leader on AI, writes in his book *Co-Intelligence: Living and Working With AI*, that researchers are finding that novices experience the greatest performance gains through the use of AI—and that we can all harness those gains by pairing our use of AI with our areas for greatest growth as professionals (a task that, itself, requires quite a bit of our own internal self-awareness).

External Self-Awareness

Moving now to external self-awareness, to the idea of AI as a mirror, we might ask students to take their insights from internal self-awareness activities—for example, an area for growth they've identified wanting to work on, such as assertiveness. We can then leverage AI through simulations and feedback protocols to provide students spaces in which to practice and receive reflections on those skills. To exemplify such a dynamic, I'm again using ChatGPT-4o, and I am again compelled to first highlight the need for careful human moderation of students' use of these tools (e.g., in search of an SEL-specific bot, I clicked "Explore GPTs" and searched the thousands of AI personae available; when I said I wanted to work on assertiveness, the first result was an AI trained in dominatrix discourse—reinforcing that, in an educational context with minors, the possibility of these tools is coupled with peril, and we need to consider both technological and instructional parameters that can help us insert guardrails—constraints for safe use in classroom contexts).

Using Self-Awareness to Spark Simulation

Working only in the standard GPT-4o space (to avoid the problematic GPTs noted previously), I prompt the AI to create a simulation scenario—which moves toward gamification theory and may, though we'll need researchers to study this, enhance student engagement. I position myself as a student and ask the AI to collect but withhold targeted feedback on my assertiveness until I'm ready for it—leveraging my internal self-awareness skills to coalesce with external:

> I'm a ninth-grade student who wants to get better at being assertive in my communication with friends, family, and professional mentors. Please create a scenario where I can practice my assertive communication skills with you. Collect feedback on how assertive I'm being but don't share that feedback until I say I'm ready for it.

The AI responds with a tailored scenario and provocation for me to engage in simulated discourse:

Scenario: Group Project Decision

You are part of a group project for your history class. Your group needs to decide on a topic for your project. You have a strong preference for a particular topic because you find it fascinating and believe it has a lot of potential for a good grade. However, one of your friends in the group has suggested a different topic that you think is less interesting and might be harder to research.

Your goal:

Communicate your preference for the topic you believe in while respecting your friend's opinion and trying to find a solution that works for everyone. Whenever you're ready, start the conversation by addressing me as one of your group members. I'll play the role of your friend who has suggested the other topic. Once you're done, let me know when you want feedback. You can start when ready!

(OpenAI, 2024)

Of course, written discourse is not the same as in-the-moment verbal engagement—but we'll soon see AI tools that involve virtual reality (VR) simulations in which such a scenario could take place through spoken discourse with digitized groupmates.

When working with students, remind them not to speak in hypotheticals—for example, responding with phrases like "I would say___." Instead, to most closely emulate real-world interaction, ask them to tailor their input as if they were indeed talking to a peer.

Doing my best to emulate a ninth grader, I engaged in the described simulation by setting forth an argument that the group history project should focus on the invention of the Internet, not the Industrial Revolution as my groupmates suggested, because our history unit focuses on more modern times. After several back-and-forths, I asked for feedback—at which point the AI told me I did a great job and pointed toward examples of why. If I were a ninth grader, I'd feel pleased and likely move on. But for the purposes of this exercise and from the vantage point of my adult brain, I prompted for constructive feedback—"How can I do better?"—at which point the AI gave me specific areas for improvement and sample text that I could've used, incorporating those suggestions:

You did a great job overall, but here are a few suggestions to further improve your assertiveness:

1. ***Use "I" Statements:*** *Using "I" statements can help you take ownership of your thoughts and feelings, which can make your communication even more assertive. For example, you could say, "I feel that the Industrial Revolution is crucial to understand modern technology," instead of "I believe that the Industrial Revolution is equally important."*
2. ***Be More Specific:*** *When discussing the pros and cons or suggesting compromises, being more specific can help clarify*

your points. For example, you might say, "One advantage of studying the Industrial Revolution is that we can understand the roots of technological advancements that led to the internet."

3. **Ask for Feedback:** *At the end of your proposal, you could ask for feedback to involve the other person in the decision-making process. For instance, "Does this approach address your concerns about the project scope?" This invites further dialogue and shows you value their input.*

4. **Express Confidence:** *While you were respectful and collaborative, you can also express a bit more confidence in your suggestions. For example, "I'm confident that incorporating both historical and modern perspectives will make our project stand out."*

Here's a revised version of your response with these improvements:

"I appreciate your passion for the Industrial Revolution—it's a fascinating period, especially in relation to climate change. I feel that focusing on a recent topic like the invention of the internet aligns well with our unit on modern times and recent history. However, I believe the Industrial Revolution is crucial to understanding how modern technological advances, including the internet, came to be.

To address both points, how about we start with a brief overview of the Industrial Revolution and then focus on its impact on the development of the internet? This way, we cover the historical context while staying relevant to our current unit. One advantage of this approach is that it highlights the continuity of technological progress.

What do you think about this compromise? Does it address your concerns about the project scope?"

(OpenAI, 2024)

To truly center the intended skill here—external self-awareness—I could revise my initial prompt in several ways: asking the AI to respond as a fellow ninth grader (its simulated responses felt a bit clunky, and certainly not true to youth voice), and I could specify that I want constructive feedback, not just praise, on my assertiveness—eliminating the need to prompt again regarding improvement. It is that constructive feedback that creates a mirror, the reflection against which to further understand, internalize, and improve my skills.

The honing of prompts in this way is called prompt engineering—however, researchers suggest that soon we will not need to prompt AI, or at least won't need to prompt it in such specific and lengthy ways, as it will be able to (statistically) guess our goals and aims and tailor feedback accordingly. Thus, prompt engineering is likely a transient skill, and while we should attune to its nuances now to drive the results we wish for—for ourselves and with students—explicitly teaching prompt crafting may not be necessary long term (Mollick, 2024).

The takeaway, then, is that simulations—which we will explore in various ways throughout this book—can target the granularities of self-awareness, a core social-emotional competency, when we use them to aid our own direct instruction and feedback regarding students' skills.

It's also important to keep in mind the central role of self-reflection in teaching, particularly in the pedagogical orientations we explore in this book—culturally responsive teaching and social-emotional learning. You might adapt these activities to support your own reflective practice or use educator-facing tools like ISTE's forthcoming Teaching Assistant chatbot to engage in Socratic or collaborative discourse with a simulated professional peer (particularly if you struggle to find colleagues who share your pedagogical ethos in your teaching community).

Social Awareness and Relationship Skills

Simulations are equally relevant when considering the more other-focused competencies in the CASEL framework: social awareness and relationship skills. Here, we might set up AI simulations that allow students to practice setting boundaries with friends; negotiating for a raise when they return to work for a second summer at their local ice cream shop; disagreeing respectfully with a future college roommate; simulating difficult conversations, perhaps about a peer's loss or mental health challenges; or intervening in a bullying situation as an active bystander. We might also use simulations to support students' third-person perspective-taking, or theory of mind (ToM)—their ability to conceptualize another person's thoughts and feelings, whether by asking the AI to prompt them or by prompting them ourselves to think and talk about how they imagine the other person thought and felt throughout the interaction and to probe their reasoning for that thinking.

From an equity standpoint, simulations may also support students' cross-cultural communication skills, though AI is trained on primarily Western, white, Eurocentric data that precludes its authentic, culturally responsive representation of diverse backgrounds, cultures, dialects, and belief systems (Buolamwini, 2023; Mollick, 2024). We should actively address this dynamic with students and leverage it for culturally responsive teaching and critical analysis. We can consider together, for example, questions like: "What makes a conversation culturally responsive? How do we know?" and "What criteria might we use to assess whether a text is culturally responsive? What research skills might we need—and what sources might we turn to—to determine how responsive a given piece of text is?," inquiries that Marlee has already addressed and provided guidance for in previous chapters.

Together, we can analyze AI misrepresentations and omissions, interrogating its biases.

You might work with your students to create, on the board or as collateral that you print and pass out to students, an "ingredients list" for culturally responsive texts and interactions—criteria against which to factually and ethically check the AI chats generated through the various simulations posited before.

Taking all of this into consideration, if we were to center relationship skills—specifically, the active bystander skills mentioned previously—we might prompt the AI:

> I'm a tenth-grade student working on my relationship skills, and I want to become an active bystander. Through a simulation, help me practice standing up for a friend in a bullying situation. Provide constructive feedback on my skills when I tell you to.

I kept this prompt simple, again attempting to emulate the minimalist style of much youth writing. ChatGPT-4o presented the following simulation:

Scenario:

You and your friend, Alex, are at school during lunch break. A group of students, led by Jordan, starts making fun of Alex's clothes, calling them "ugly" and "out of style." Alex looks visibly upset but doesn't say anything. The other students are laughing and encouraging Jordan to continue.

Your Turn:

1. ***Identify the Bullying:*** *You recognize that Alex is being bullied.*
2. ***Assess the Situation:*** *Decide whether it is safe to intervene directly or if you should seek help from a teacher or another trusted adult.*
3. ***Take Action:*** *Choose one or more of the following options to intervene:*

    ♦ *Directly address the bully.*
    ♦ *Support your friend Alex.*
    ♦ *Distract the bully.*
    ♦ *Seek help.*

When you're ready, describe how you would respond in this situation. After you do, I'll provide feedback on your response.

(OpenAI, 2024)

I appreciate the sequential approach, the step-by-step nature of the guidance, and the choose-your-own-adventure style of the third step, which gives students multiple entry points—requiring them to practice their self-awareness, social awareness, and responsible decision-making skills, all tenets of CASEL's framework.

As facilitators, we would remind students to respond directly to the AI as if it were Jordan, the bully, to reap the benefits of simulation (Mollick, 2024)—rather than use hypothetical "I would. . ." language. To infuse the activity with a culturally responsive educational approach, we might prompt students to consider additional identity-based dynamics not articulated in the AI example—in what ways might class, gender, race, ability, or other identifiers impact this scenario? How do the identities of Jordan, Alex, and the student entering the scene as an active bystander—similarities and differences—impact how they choose to move forward in the third action-oriented section of this provocation? What power dynamics are at play in bullying scenarios, and how do they reflect—or how are they informed by—broader sociopolitical landscapes in our educational, local, national, and global environments?

A great visual for encouraging students to think about the intersections of these environmental influences is that of Urie Bronfenbrenner's bioecological systems theory of development, which offers a concentric circle diagram depicting how our various environments intertwine, how even one-on-one interactions are microcosms reflective of broader influences. For easy access to this visual, visit www.simplypsychology.org/bronfenbrenner.html (Cherry, 2023; Guy-Evans, 2024).

In the scenario presented, you might invite students to engage in multiple simulations, building upon the initial interaction in several ways:

1. Invite students to follow each of the proposed interventional paths to see how they turn out. Which approaches feel most effective and most challenging for them? Ask them to write and/or talk about why they had these reactions, again practicing internal self-awareness.
2. Ask students to take Implicit Association Tests (IATs) from Harvard University's Project Implicit (available at https://implicit.harvard.edu/implicit/takeatest.html) to identify and reflect on their own internal biases (2011). After engaging with these tests and writing and talking about their results with peers and as a group, invite students to return to the bullying scenario considering how characters' identifiers may impact their own actions based on their implicit biases. Ask them to consider strategies for counteracting those biases—rooted in this scenario but, of course, applying more broadly to their interpersonal skills and relationships.

3. Position them to practice perspective-taking and self-awareness by asking them to consider, if they were in a position of needing an active bystander, which approach would they most appreciate their witness taking? Why? What verbal and nonverbal approaches make them feel most supported, most safe?

This scenario is just one of the many simulations possible when using AI to support students' social awareness and relationship skills; consider polling your class for real-world examples they would most like to work on (such as the college- and job-related scenes mentioned at the start of this section, culturally responsive conversations with peers around the world, navigating a political conversation with someone of an opposing viewpoint, and more). Then, set up GPTs to re-create those moments digitally, presenting the choose-your-own-adventure structure that this example provides.

At the conclusion of a simulation, leverage the power of human interaction by engaging in reflective writing, think-pair-share activities, and whole–group discussions using questions like the following:

1. What did you find most helpful and most challenging about the simulation, and why?
2. Using the class "ingredients list" for culturally responsive interaction, do you feel this dialogue was culturally responsive? How could it be more so?
3. What did you learn about yourself throughout this simulation?
4. How might you apply this simulation to real-world interactions within the next (day, week, semester)?
5. What transferable skills can you identify in this simulation—meaning skills you can apply to other contexts and scenarios?

6. What goal(s) do you have for yourself to continue honing your social awareness and relationship skills related to this type of interaction?

You might also invite students to share summaries of their inputs and to identify similarities and differences in their approaches, combining and learning from class experiences to set collective goals.

Self-Management and Responsible Decision-Making

As is likely obvious in the preceding sections, social-emotional competencies are not mutually exclusive. One cannot practice relationship skills without also activating self-awareness and, in many cases, responsible decision-making. Considering the remaining two competencies in the framework, though—indeed, responsible decision-making, as well as self-management—we consider the complexities of operationalizing our self-awareness and social skills to regulate how we show up in the world, how we govern our lives, and how we choose to relate to others. Using AI, we might first support self-management in several ways.

Executive Functioning Supports

Executive functioning skills (EFs)—the ability to make plans and schedules, filter distractions, hold information in one's working memory, and prioritize tasks and information (Center on the Developing Child, 2024)—are skills that students must learn and that are dependent upon one's habits, surroundings, and stress levels. As you likely know, many students (and adults!) struggle with these skills for myriad reasons, whether due to a neurological condition like attention deficit hyperactivity disorder (ADHD) or early childhood trauma, which can change the brain in ways that impact these functions (Administration for Children & Families, 2024). So, the prospect of a tool that makes these skills more attainable offers a boon.

Simulations—described in detail before—also apply here. For example, you might set up simulations for students to practice making responsible decisions in the face of competing priorities. Or, you might support their impulse control by building into AI simulations moments of pause—signaling the AI to suggest a break when the student seems to be getting distracted, frustrated, or otherwise disengaged, and to provide a list of possible break activities (e.g., deep breathing, counting to 10, walking around the room, responding to a reflective journaling prompt). It's worth noting, too, that using AI supports and requires students' responsible decision-making—their deciding whether and when to use AI tools, to do so in ethical and honest ways, and to fact-check and engage in critical literacy are all responsible decisions that we can help them learn to make.

But returning to the idea of executive functioning and the self-management inherent in these and other competencies, there are several ways you might position AI to support students' EFs.

Backward Planning

While ChapGPT can create schedules and to-do lists, its educational power is in its ability to guide students toward their own executive functioning processes. For example, students might have an ongoing thread open in ChatGPT that helps them backward plan for a big assignment. Inputting the deadline and assignment details, the student might ask the AI to guide them in creating a plan to tackle the assignment in small chunks over the course of two weeks. Each day, the student can log progress in this digital notebook space and work with the AI bot to update the two-week plan accordingly. Doing so offers a dynamic visual and textual map that is updated in the moment. Or the student might ask for three different possible work cadences, then have an opportunity to compare and contrast which works best for them—understanding at the outset the ramifications of each, like fewer, longer working sessions versus many shorter bursts of studying.

Time Management and Routine

As with backward planning, ChatGPT can support other types of time management and the creation of daily routines. Many students struggle with prioritization, for example, and can ask the AI to serve as a coach and guide them in the creation of a homework to-do list. After they enter their various assignments, the AI can prompt them to consider the pros, cons, time requirements, and deadlines of each, co-creating a to-do list that is accordingly aligned.

Or let's say a student needs to better integrate their various extracurriculars into a schedule that includes homework, socialization, and family time. You might help them use ChatGPT and Google calendar side-by-side to automate reminders and time block their days, with an ongoing ChatGPT space where, again, they can share daily updates and reapportion their calendar as new needs arise. You might include in the instructions to ChatGPT the directive to prompt students to engage in constructive self-reflection when they make changes to the schedule or to input notes about how their time management went that day—what about the plan worked, what they had to adjust, and how they navigated any unexpected changes—to reinforce internal self-awareness; you and the student can review this log together in one-on-one conferencing. This type of in-the-moment data collection allows a more comprehensive look into students' days, their executive functioning, and skill development than previous calendaring and journaling tools have, meaning we will have more information with which to better support and scaffold their growth.

Mindfulness

"Engaging in short-term meditation practice improves executive function, as measured by performance on the Stroop task," write researchers Teper and Inzlicht (2013, p. 85), referring to a common neurocognitive test that measures attention and information processing (Ruhl, 2018). Though they sometimes gets a bad reputation for being too aligned with performative self-care in pop-psychology circles, mindfulness and meditation have real power to change the brain, support mental health, and boost executive functioning. But not every teacher feels qualified to guide students in mindfulness practices, which is where AI can come in.

Though we can introduce students to guided meditations or body scans, it's more personal and relational to facilitate mindfulness activities ourselves, building community and modeling participation rather than outsourcing the activity to a YouTube video. ChatGPT can provide the script. I input, for example, the following scenario:

> Please design a five-minute guided meditation for a group of ninth and tenth-graders. They are new to meditation and many feel resistant to it. We will be practicing at the start of a school assembly, and we will ask students to repeat the practice on their own after school.

In response, I received a detailed script tailored to the context, which I might read aloud and then distribute to students for individual and repeated practice; I also received some practical tips for teachers:

Introduction (1 minute)

"Good morning, everyone. Today, we're going to try something a little different to help us all start the day with a clear mind and calm energy. I know some of you might feel unsure or even a bit skeptical about meditation, but I invite you to give

it a try. Think of it as a way to reset and recharge your brain, just like rebooting your phone when it's acting up."

Preparation (1 minute)

1. ***Get Comfortable:*** "First, let's all get comfortable. Sit up straight in your chairs with your feet flat on the floor. Rest your hands on your lap or your knees, whatever feels most natural."
2. ***Close Your Eyes:*** "Now, gently close your eyes. If you don't feel comfortable closing your eyes, just lower your gaze to the floor."
3. ***Breathe Deeply:*** "Take a deep breath in through your nose, hold it for a moment, and then slowly exhale through your mouth. Let's do that two more times."

Main Meditation (2 minutes)

1. ***Focus on Breathing:*** "Now, let's settle into a natural breathing rhythm. Just breathe in and out through your nose, nice and easy. Don't worry about changing your breath, just notice it. Feel the air coming in, filling up your lungs, and then flowing out."
2. ***Body Awareness:*** "As you keep breathing, bring your attention to your body. Start with your feet. Notice how they feel on the ground. Move your attention slowly up your legs, to your knees, thighs, and so on, all the way up to the top of your head. If you notice any areas of tension, just imagine that area relaxing."
3. ***Mindfulness:*** "Now, let's focus on just being here in this moment. If your mind starts to wander, that's okay. Just gently bring your focus back to your breath. Remember, there's no right or wrong way to feel. Just be present."

Closing (1 minute)

1. ***Gradual Return:*** "We're almost done. Start to bring your awareness back to the room. Notice any sounds you might hear around you. Feel the chair under you and the floor beneath your feet."

2. ***Open Your Eyes:*** *"When you're ready, take another deep breath, and as you exhale, gently open your eyes."*
3. ***Reflection:*** *"Take a moment to notice how you feel right now. You might feel a little more relaxed or calm. Remember, you can do this anytime you need a break or a moment of peace. Thanks for giving it a try."*

Encouragement for Personal Practice

"After school, try to find a quiet spot for just a few minutes to practice this again. It can be a great way to unwind after a busy day. And remember, it's okay if it feels a little strange at first. The more you practice, the easier it becomes."

Tips for Teachers

- ***Set the Tone:*** *Before starting, make sure the environment is as quiet as possible. Dim the lights if you can, and ensure that all distractions are minimized.*
- ***Encourage Openness:*** *Remind students that it's okay if their minds wander, and the goal is not to achieve a perfect meditation but to simply practice being present.*
- ***Consistency:*** *Suggest that students try to incorporate this practice into their daily routine, perhaps right after school or before bedtime.*

By introducing meditation in a gentle and encouraging manner, you can help students discover a valuable tool for managing stress and enhancing their well-being.

(OpenAI, 2024)

Other tools, like Vital, a generative AI tool that generates meditations based on your emotions and contexts (accessible at https://joinvital.ai/), are further expanding the ways in which we can introduce students to mindfulness in ways that feel individualized.

What's more, "in addition to creating personalized meditations, AI can also be used to track and measure the effectiveness of meditation practice," writes AI blogger Kevin Menear (2023):

> With the use of wearables and other technology, AI can provide real-time feedback on the body's physiological response to meditation. This can help meditators better understand their own practice and make adjustments as needed. As AI continues to evolve, the possibilities for using it in meditation are endless. From virtual reality meditation experiences to AI-powered mindfulness coaches, the future of meditation is looking more and more technologically advanced.
>
> (p. 1)

As with other social-emotional learning tasks, time burden is a frequent barrier to teachers' engaging students in this type of work. With the ability to produce content tailored to students' contexts, personalities, and preferences in under a minute, it's feasible that teachers can now begin to incorporate more socially and emotionally supportive practices, like mindfulness, without adding more planning time to their plates.

To recap, you can engage AI tools to enhance SEL in the following ways:

Box 3.1 AI Usage and Benefits With Regard to Social-Emotional Learning

- Use AI to help students practice metacognition, targeting internal and external self-awareness through reflection prompts.
- Leverage AI to create simulations that safely and responsively provide students opportunities to practice social awareness and relationship skills.
- Use AI as a jumping-off point to discuss—live with students—what it means to make responsible decisions as a digital citizen.

- Use AI to support students' executive functioning skills, tailoring chats according to individual students' needs and areas for growth.
- Leverage AI as an organizational tool, for yourself and with students, to scaffold processes like backward-planning, goal-setting, and more.
- Combat time burden by using generative AI to help you incorporate activities and pedagogies you may not otherwise have time for, such as meditation through customized scripts or journaling through prompts attuned to students' interests.
- Connect SEL, culturally responsive teaching, and AI by building into these activities practices that involve interrogating AI outputs for responsiveness; considering the role of positionalities and systems; and analyzing bias (such as in the implicit bias extension activity from before).

Box 3.2 Try Out the Tech and Reflect

Take a moment to practice your own internal self-awareness skills; considering the various use cases outlined throughout this chapter, from executive functioning to metacognitive writing to implicit bias analysis, select one that you feel you would most benefit from practicing. In a new ChatGPT thread, practice the exercise yourself—whether backward planning a lesson, simulating a tough conversation with a colleague (akin to the bullying scenario described in this chapter), or asking for feedback on a social-emotional skill you aim to hone, from assertiveness to empathy to open-ended questioning.

Take 10–15 minutes to engage with the AI on this particular area of focus, and consider: How authentic does the interaction feel? Does your connection to the AI shift or change throughout the course of the activity, and if so, in what ways? What feelings do you have in reaction to this exercise? What thoughts or analyses do you have? How might this first-person experience inform your use of AI in similar ways with your students?

References

Administration for Children & Families. (2024). *Executive function*. www.acf.hhs.gov/trauma-toolkit/executive-function

Brough, E. (2023, July 14). Research finds social and emotional learning produces significant benefits for students. *Yale School of Medicine*. https://medicine.yale.edu/news-article/new-research-published-in-child-development-confirms-social-and-emotional-learning-significantly-improves-student-academic-performance-well-being-and-perceptions-of-school-safety/

Buolamwini, J. (2023). *Unmasking AI: My mission to protect what is human in a world of machines*. Random House.

CASEL. (2023, March 3). *What is the CASEL framework*? https://casel.org/fundamentals-of-sel/what-is-the-casel-framework/

Center on the Developing Child. (2024). *What is executive function? And how does it relate to child development*? https://harvardcenter.wpenginepowered.com/wp-content/uploads/2019/04/ExecutiveFunctionInfographic_FINAL.pdf

Cherry, K. (2023, August 16). A comprehensive guide to the Bronfenbrenner ecological model. *Verywell Mind*. www.verywellmind.com/bronfenbrenner-ecological-model-7643403

Cipriano, C., Strambler, M. J., Naples, L., Ha, C., Kirk, M. A., Wood, M. E., Sehgal, K., Zieher, A. K., Eveleigh, A., McCarthy, M. F., Funaro, M. C., Ponnock, A., Chow, J., & Durlak, J. (2023). The state of the evidence for social and emotional learning: A contemporary meta-analysis of universal school-based SEL interventions. *Child Development*, 94(5), 1181–1204. https://doi.org/10.31219/osf.io/mk35u

Collins, B. R. (2024, January 29). Opinion: Teachers and students are not okay right now. More mental health training would help.

The Hechinger Report. https://hechingerreport.org/opinion-teachers-and-students-are-not-okay-right-now-more-mental-health-training-would-help/

Durlak, J. A., Weissberg, R. P., Dymnicki, A. B., Taylor, R. D., & Schellinger, K. B. (2011). The impact of enhancing students' social and emotional learning: A meta-analysis of school-based universal interventions. *Child Development, 82*(1), 405–432. https://doi.org/10.1111/j.1467-8624.2010.01564.x

Eurich, T. (2018, January 4). What self-awareness really is (and how to cultivate it). *Harvard Business Review.* https://hbr.org/2018/01/what-self-awareness-really-is-and-how-to-cultivate-it

Guy-Evans, O. (2024, January 17). Bronfenbrenner's ecological systems theory. *Simply Psychology.* www.simplypsychology.org/bronfenbrenner.html

Harvard Graduate School of Education. (2015). I used to think . . . now I think . . . *Project Zero.* https://pz.harvard.edu/resources/i-used-to-think-now-i-think

Harvard University. (2011). Project implicit. *Take a Test.* https://implicit.harvard.edu/implicit/takeatest.html

Lin, L., Parker, K., & Horowitz, J. M. (2024, April 4). What's it like to be a teacher in America today? *Pew Research Center.* www.pewresearch.org/social-trends/2024/04/04/whats-it-like-to-be-a-teacher-in-america-today/

Menear, K. (2023, March 9). Mind and machine: How AI is enhancing the meditation experience by personalizing the path to inner peace. *Medium.* https://medium.com/@kevin.menear/mind-and-machine-how-ai-is-enhancing-the-meditation-experience-by-personalizing-the-path-to-inner-46ab6a5ab7ae

Mollick, E. (2024). *Co-intelligence: Living and working with AI.* Portfolio/Penguin.

OpenAI. (2024). *ChatGPT* (Jan 8 version) [Large language model]. https://chat.openai.com/chat

Ruhl, C. (2018). *Stroop effect.* Simply Psychology. https://www.simplypsychology.org/stroop-effect.html

SAMHSA. (2024). *Understanding child trauma.* www.samhsa.gov/child-trauma/understanding-child-trauma

Schimelpfening, N. (2023, March 13). Stress can affect your ability to think clearly, study finds. *Healthline*. www.healthline.com/health-news/why-it-may-be-harder-to-make-good-decisions-when-your-stressed

Solis, M. (2024, February 15). 'There is not enough of me to go around': Schools need more counselors. *National Education Association*. https://www.nea.org/nea-today/all-news-articles/schools-need-more-counselors

Strobbe, K. (2021, August 3). Windows, mirrors, and sliding glass doors. *Working in the Schools*. https://witschicago.org/windows-mirrors-and-sliding-glass-doors

Teicher, M. H., Samson, J. A., Anderson, C. M., & Ohashi, K. (2016). The effects of childhood maltreatment on brain structure, function and connectivity. *Nature Reviews Neuroscience*, *17*(10), 652–666. https://doi.org/10.1038/nrn.2016.111

Teper, R., & Inzlicht, M. (2013). Meditation, mindfulness and executive control: The importance of emotional acceptance and brain-based performance monitoring. *Social Cognitive and Affective Neuroscience*, *8*(1), 85–92. https://doi.org/10.1093/scan/nss045

Walker, T. (2024). What teachers want the public to know. *NEA*. www.nea.org/nea-today/all-news-articles/what-teachers-want-public-know

World Health Organization. (2024). Mental health of adolescents. *World Health Organization*. www.who.int/news-room/fact-sheets/detail/adolescent-mental-health

Poetic Reflection

How to Begin

Jordan Stempleman

What ends in an argument
can't be called feedback.
It's like taking a writing class
in the food court with a sea
of teenagers who break up with one another
as you grind a blank Word document
into dust.
Yesterday, I thought I'd never write again.
Today, I write again, but again
means something more
like an exaggeration
of what it felt like not to write yesterday.
Am I writing again because I used the snowblower
two mornings in a row?
Or is it because on the second morning, after the snow
blew back into my face, my neighbor
walked over and said, "That thing
sounds like it's going to bust a rod."
And afterward, I thought, expertise
has a diction the present rarely tolerates.
I begin to write--*today, I thought*--and then listen, as I imagine
one listens, eating walnuts just out of view.

4

Using AI to Integrate Cultural Responsiveness and SEL Into English Language Arts

Brittany R. Collins

"As a student who wishes to continue writing, I have worried about what the professional world will look like if I have to compete with or work alongside AI," wrote teenage author Cameron Alleyne in a blog post for Write the World, Inc., in July, 2024. "It has left me to question what role the arts will have in our world by the time I'm an adult since anyone has the power to create using AI" (Alleyne, 2024, p. 1).

I had the privilege of working with Cameron during her tenure as a teen AI liaison tasked with researching and reporting on emerging AI innovations and use cases for students, writers, and teachers, sharing her perspective as a high school student with the nonprofit's global audience. Throughout her research, Cameron expressed concerns about the equity implications of AI, from perpetuating and spreading misinformation, to making rampant the sexualization of young women through deepfakes, to plagiarism, and more. As an aspiring author, she found that the generative nature of AI particularly concerned her, and many writers relate. However, her thinking shifted toward a "both/and" perspective, as she articulated in one of her posts, writing:

DOI: 10.4324/9781003510291-5

I've realized that AI's abilities don't have to threaten writers. Instead, they can complement or build upon existing work. AI lacks human experiences and emotions. Writers lack the expansive database and rapid pace that AI possesses. Together, with people being the leading force, AI doesn't have to be frightening. Instead, it can fit a niche in the writing world as a tool and not a replacement.

(2024, p. 1)

In secondary English language arts instruction, identifying ways to use AI "as a tool and not a replacement" seems the central task. After all, the discipline strives to help students meet authentic reading, writing, speaking, and listening objectives set by the Common Core State Standards Initiative (2024), meaning English teachers are uniquely tasked with teaching skills that, now, AI can mostly replicate.

Or can it?

Storytelling is a deeply human skill (Gottschall, 2013), and Marlee outlined its importance in previous chapters. When we read or listen to a story, our brains produce oxytocin, a neurochemical that creates feelings of empathy and attachment, and that promotes prosocial action—so much so that researchers have termed it "the moral molecule" (Zak, 2012). And storytelling is vast—from reading a picture book to orating a cultural myth, sharing a family story, responding to an interviewer's probe (e.g., "Tell me about yourself"), advocating for a family member's health needs, buying a car, explaining a product to a customer—nearly every facet of our lives is bound up in narrative. So, storytelling is not superfluous and neither is it only about reading and writing but rather the complex cognitive processes implicated in those tasks—like self-reflection, identifying a goal, intuiting the positionalities of one's intended audience, distilling information into its most pertinent points, attuning to emotional impacts and intents, accounting for counterarguments, tracking one's growth across time, refining one's content through iterative revision, and so much more.

All of these skills inherently involve social-emotional competencies (all five tenets of the CASEL framework previously named) and cultural responsiveness. And they demonstrate that the processes at the heart of ELA instruction are just that—processes—that possess their own learning merits arguably more important than the value of any one particular writing product.

Can AI technology now generate that same product at lightning speed? Yes. But learners lose the inquiry, reflection, and innovation—the deep cognitive work, the idea of writing *as* thinking—when outsourcing their processes to a machine. In this chapter, we'll explore how ELA teachers can preserve the power and importance of authentic creative and analytical writing processes while using AI technologies to support and even enhance them—attuning, at the same time, to SEL and equity-centered teaching practices.

Simulating Intended Audiences

In writing, audience plays a central role—yet authentic audiences are too often missing from classroom-based instruction. In the "real" world, authors must identify the central objective of their work and the main message that they strive to communicate. They need to know whom they most hope to deliver that message to, and why: Are they working to convince naysayers, to evoke laughter and levity, or to pay tribute to a cultural legacy? What identities, belief systems, language(s), and life experiences do their audience members hold, how do those elements influence their audience members' perspectives and preferences, and how might all of that information influence the writer's technical decisions—from the tone of their writing, to their diction, syntax, cultural references/allusions, citations, and more?

In the classroom, however, students spend little time writing; NAEP data reveal that "just a quarter of students in middle school and high school write for at least 30 minutes a day, a minimum standard set by learning experts for the development of writing skills" (Schaffhauser, 2020, p. 1; Picou, 2023). This paucity is important, given that only 24% of middle and high school students demonstrated proficient writing skills on the last national assessment, with proficiency remaining unchanged as students progressed through high school (NAEP, 2012). These data suggest an urgent need for more time dedicated to skill-building and practice.

And even when students do write, their processes rarely reflect real-world work; that's because ELA curricula often present writing as a linear, stage-by-stage process, typically involving one round of revision (usually focused on line edits), with the sole audience being a student's teacher (and perhaps one peer, who may provide line edits prior to final submission); the central goal is a grade (Collins, 2024a). This linearity misrepresents the often messy, iterative processes involved in authentic writing tasks. Usually, these tasks require multiple rounds of revision at both "macro" and "micro" levels, through developmental and copy edits that involve social interactions between the author and multiple readers. Ultimately, these interactions allow the writer to better reach their readers and achieve a prescient goal, whether persuasion or education or entertainment.

When writing instruction lacks real-world relevance and oversimplifies the writing process, it can become rote—disengaging to students, which further erodes their performance.

That's where intended audiences come in.

It may not be feasible to connect student writers with their real intended audiences for every writing assignment—much as it should be a goal to create opportunities to share youth voices with the world, whether through student publications, local newspapers, area poetry slams, rallies for social causes, or other meaningful venues. For that reason, though, might we make writing feel more authentic and meaningful—and make the sensation of audience more accessible—through AI simulations?

By encouraging students to identify an audience other than their teacher, to compose a piece with that audience in mind, and to receive feedback from that audience—as a supplement to peer and educator feedback—might we deepen engagement, provide more time-on-task practice, and perhaps boost their proficiency?

And, understanding that an audience may not be a monolith, might we encourage through such simulations social-emotional skills like perspective-taking (a competency further honed during adolescent brain development [Nakkula & Toshalis, 2020]), social awareness, and theory of mind, or "the ability to attribute mental states, including emotions, desires, beliefs, and knowledge, and recognize that other people's thoughts and beliefs may differ from yours" (Cherry, 2023, p. 1)?

To cultivate these skills, you might take a three-pronged approach to using AI with students:

Box 4.1 Using AI to Simulate an Intended Audience

Step 1: Identity Map. Before considering how one's intended audience might impact the composition of a piece of writing, an author must first understand their own identity, perspective, and positionality—who they are, what they believe in, and why.

This type of identity work is also at the core of culturally responsive teaching and targets the social-emotional competency of self-awareness. To ignite intended audience activities in your classroom, first engage students in an identity mapping activity; there are many available online, but I particularly appreciate that of Facing History and Ourselves, which you can access at this URL (though you could prompt AI to help students create identity maps, too): www.facinghistory.org/resource-library/identity-charts-0

In this activity, students think about the various identifiers, social positions, and life experiences that comprise their identities; they create both visual and written representations of their identities. These maps help them consider which facets of their identities give them privilege, which are minoritized, and how their various "parts" coalesce into their whole, intersectional identity.

You might use these maps to facilitate a conversation about identity "salience," introducing the idea that different parts of our identities become more dominant in certain environments—for example, a Black trans student in a white-majority class may feel that race is their most salient identifier at school but that their gender is most salient at home, where they haven't yet come out to their parents and carry the weight of a secret.

Of course, identity map activities should be challenge-by-choice, and students should have agency over whether and with whom they choose to share them. But even if limited to self-practice, this activity can increase self-awareness and help students understand the lens through which they see the world as writers.

Another engaging identity-based writing activity that you might use as an extension to identity mapping is the "Where I'm From" poem. Writers model the work of poet George Ella Lyon, creating poetry that describes, in rich sensory detail, the people, places, experiences, sounds, and surroundings that have made the writer who they are. For more information, check out the I Am From Project at www.georgeellalyon.com/where.html

Step 2: Create a Written Portrait of an Intended Audience Member. You might prompt students to create an identity map, a hypothetical "Where I'm From" poem, or a narrative portrait (such as a vignette or character description) for a member of their imagined intended audience to further concretize that audience—their beliefs, backgrounds, quirks, motivations—in writers' minds. Doing so additionally reinforces students' theory of mind, described before, bolstering social-emotional learning.

Once students have created the map, ask them to place it side-by-side with their own and, with a highlighter or marker, to circle similarities and star differences. You might offer reflection questions as they prepare to write, regarding how knowledge of these similarities and differences will inform their decision-making as writers: What barriers might they need to overcome to appeal to their audience? What similarities might they reference to find common ground or to deepen their emotional or logical appeal?

Step 3: Prompt the AI. Once they have a more nuanced understanding of their intended audience from the identity-mapping/portraiture activity above, it's time for students to prompt the AI tool of their choice, such as ChatGPT, to simulate that audience member and to engage in a feedback process regarding the student's writing.

For example, a student writing an opinion essay with the central argument that their town officials need to do more to prevent discriminatory housing practices impacting BIPOC and LGBTQIA+ individuals might select a city councilor as an intended audience member. They can research this individual's background and work trajectory, the policies that they have advocated for or worked to enact, and other pertinent details, and then use that information to tell the AI about whom it's emulating.

Students should also be specific about the type of feedback that they seek—should the AI-simulated audience member comment on tone, for example, or convincingness of argument, or evidence, or something else entirely? Providing directions of this sort requires metacognition, encouraging students to think about their own thinking and writing through an analytical lens, to identify strengths and areas for growth, and to set an objective and work toward it in their writing.

Step 4: Reflect and Revise. Encourage students to engage directly with their simulated intended audience member as if in a chatroom with the real person. In the example, rather than receive one round of feedback, the student should engage in dialogic discourse with the simulated city councilor about the style or content of their writing, to further develop and hone their thinking, which they will then have a record of and can integrate in revision.

To achieve speaking and listening standards, students can also use emerging voice capabilities to speak aloud to/with AI tools, moving from page to emulated stage as they practice performing, debating, or educating a simulated audience aloud (before, ideally, then reenacting that work for a peer, the class, or a broader audience).

After this activity, ask your students to think, write, and/or talk in response to reflection questions such as: How authentic did the interaction feel? What are your takeaways? What did you feel most proud of throughout the interaction, and what are you now motivated to change or work on? Are there any other intended audience members you now wish to engage with through simulation, who might offer a different vantage point on the same piece of work? How do your identity as a writer/speaker and the identity of your simulated audience member influence this interaction and the impact of the writing on both parties? What did you learn about yourself as a writer throughout this process?

By simulating intended audience members and engaging in this critical reflection, students are better positioned to make responsible decisions in their writing and to have greater social awareness as they share it, targeting two additional SEL competencies while simultaneously honing literacy.

Supporting Peer Feedback Activities

On a sunny, cool morning in early September, I met with a cohort of middle and high school students participating in a youth leadership opportunity called the Community Ambassador program at Write the World, Inc. A central task of the Community Ambassador role is to provide supportive, constructive peer reviews to other young writers around the world. So, our sessions often involve discussions about how to provide feedback that honors the writer's vision and identity and takes into consideration the *context* of a global learning community that comprises writers ages 12 to 19, publishing in a wide array of genres, from poetry to science fiction to opinion journalism. Reviewers must therefore have the agility to engage a broad technical toolbox, commenting on rhyme scheme and scansion, then counterargument, then worldbuilding. But more than that, they must be adept at navigating the subterranean layer of the reviewer-writer relationship, which includes skills like:

- Perspective-taking
- Intuiting a writer's intent and motivation
- Having empathy for the vulnerability inherent in the writing process
- Providing constructive feedback in a way that the writer will be able to receive it, such as by centering inquiry and posing ideas rather than edicts
- Focusing one's feedback on just one or two core takeaways and/or next steps, so as not to inundate the writer
- Navigating differences in ideology, identity, culture, geography, background, or experience between writer and reviewer
- Building a sense of camaraderie, support, and coalition—working with the writer as a team member, toward a common goal

This list is non-exhaustive, but each of these competencies strikes at both social-emotional and cultural competence. Craft knowledge will help one succeed on a standardized test, but to make real change through literacy and communication, one must also develop these pro-social skills.

At the opening of our meeting, during a general check-in, one young writer shared, just a few weeks into her term: "I never expected my experience as a reviewer to help me as a writer. I'm now taking the advice I'm giving other writers and applying it to my own work."

Reflexivity. Metacognition. The simultaneous, reciprocal development of core academic competencies and human-centered skills. All of this felt stunningly encapsulated in this young writer's comment.

So what role, I found myself wondering, could AI possibly play in this landscape of literacy development, when human connection was already catalyzing such powerful learning?

Though I feel protective of the relational and academic engagement inherent in peer feedback activities, it is plausible that mindful incorporation of AI feedback tools in literacy instruction can enhance accessibility and, therefore, amplify the efficacy of human peer review in the classroom—offering a scaffold, not a replacement, for meaningful student-to-student interactions.

First-Round Feedback

As I say at the start of any class, writing—no matter the genre—is a vulnerable act. Putting one's thoughts and feelings into words and then sharing those expressions with others takes great trust and courage. There are many students for whom this act causes worry. Maybe a student is penning a personal narrative about navigating opposing political viewpoints at family dinners and is concerned about what their peer reviewers' reactions will be, or an English language learner strives to smooth their grammar and mechanics before passing their work to a peer, or a student with a language-based learning disability doesn't feel that their written story accurately communicates their emotions.

Across these situations, students may benefit from having an opportunity to position an AI chatbot as a peer reviewer—prompting the tool to guide their thinking through open-ended questions and/or provide feedback on areas that the writer hopes to hone. Doing so can facilitate a practice run, providing an opportunity for the writer to engage in dialogue about their piece while preserving the metacognitive processes involved in review (by way of prompting, in which the writer still must reflect, practice self-awareness, and set an objective for the feedback). The intent, here, is not to forgo human review but to create safe spaces for writers to work through any anticipatory anxieties about that review, iterating in advance of sharing their work with a real reader.

Many AI tools exist to provide guided feedback, such as Khan Academy's Khanmigo, Grammarly's AI Writing Assistant,

Anthropic's Claude AI, and more. Student writers can also prompt a general AI chatbot, like ChatGPT, to respond to them as a peer reviewer by using framing that introduces their positionalities and objectives. Doing so might also allow them to make relevant disclosures that they may not immediately feel comfortable sharing with a human peer.

For example, extending the example provided above, a student might prompt the AI:

> *I'm a 10th grade student writing a personal narrative about my family's opposing political views. I'm an English language learner and hope to improve my use of grammar and mechanics. I'm concerned about how human readers will perceive my family members' perspectives and opinions, so I want feedback on how I portray them as characters. Respond to me as a tutor, using a mix of supportive and constructive feedback, especially through guiding questions.*

Comparative Analysis of Feedback Types

When ChatGPT was first released, its introduction into literacy classrooms (if it wasn't entirely banned) typically involved a comparative analysis assignment in which teachers asked students to compare AI feedback with human feedback on a given piece of writing, often pointing out holes in the AI critique, affirming the sometimes ineffable, sometimes definable qualities that make human reviewers especially impactful.

But what if, now that AI is a more concrete reality in many of our work and learning spaces, we moved beyond this binary either-or, good-bad approach and instead invoked as many voices as possible in the writing classroom? Would this allow students to practice the skill of synthesizing external feedback while keeping true to the integrity of their own creative vision and voice?

We can begin by structuring comparative analyses of feedback types in the following ways:

Box 4.2 Activities to Support Students' Comparative Analyses of Feedback Types in Writing Instruction

✏ Activity #1: The Committee of Three. Invite students to select a draft and prompt an AI tool for feedback, sharing their vision/goals/concerns to focus the lens of the review, as described before. Then, invite students to "prompt" their human peer reviewer(s) and teacher(s) in a similar way, letting them in on their process, focusing their engagement with the written work, and framing the lens through which they should provide feedback.

Students will receive a minimum of three reviews in this scenario—from AI, from at least one peer, and from their instructor. Invite them to think, talk, and write about the similarities and differences that they notice between and across review types. What does and doesn't feel constructive in each review type, and why? Which review type most closely aligns with their "prompt" to reviewers? What patterns, questions, or perspectives particularly stand out in each review, and why?

✏ Activity #2: Feedback, Squared. Dr. Nancy Sommers, literacy education thought leader and professor at the Harvard Graduate School of Education, writes in her book *Responding to Student Writers* about the utility of students' providing feedback on feedback:

> At various points in the term, ask students to reread and analyze your comments and to give you feedback about them. Ask students to tell you which comments are useful and why, which are not and why, and what they've learned from your comments
>
> (2013, p. 11)

Rather than pitting one type of feedback against another, you might invite students to write such a reflective memo in response to all three pieces of feedback in the example. Invite them to consider, again, what similarities and differences they notice, this time between and across their reflective feedback memos in response to these various types of feedback. How does their tone or approach change depending on which reviewer they're responding to—peer, teacher, AI? Why might these differences occur, and what can students learn from them? (Questions like these strike at the idea of intended audience and cultivate the perspective-taking inherent in social-emotional and cultural competencies.)

To encourage dialogue, you might then invite students to share their reflective memos with the reviewers themselves—extending discourse through one-on-one conferencing with an educator, peer discussion with a fellow student reviewer, and written or verbal chats with an AI bot, recursively tracking and analyzing the differences, connections, and usefulness of each unfolding conversation.

Activity #3: Expanding the Toolbox. Synthesizing their experiences from the previous activities, invite students to talk as a class, compare their experiences, and attempt to create bulleted lists (on the board or in a shared class document) about the pros, cons, and possibilities of each review type—a guide they can turn to when working on future drafts to determine which type(s) of feedback they might solicit at different stages in their writing process.

Perhaps, for example, AI reviews allow them to gain simulated feedback from a reader with a different political viewpoint or cultural or linguistic background (albeit limited, as we've previously documented how AI itself is trained on data that perpetuates systemic inequities)—a perspective they don't have access to in their classroom.

Alternatively, maybe feedback from a peer helps them feel more supported and motivated to keep writing, since they know that person well, or because their peer review interactions helped them to connect, and now they sit together at the lunch table and have fostered a friendship. And perhaps educator feedback helps a student best plan for their summative assessment or to imagine applying their writing in college or career.

Casting these feedback types as resources at young writers' disposal, while pushing students to think critically about each, expands their toolboxes and self- and social awareness, core social-emotional skills. Rather than strive to determine which feedback type "wins," we can instead broaden the arena of perspectives, both simulated and real, that students may access as they develop their own authentic voices. This theater-in-the-round approach can help them identify blindspots, gain confidence, and later transfer the skill of synthesis to feedback exercises in professional and personal contexts alike.

Box 4.3 💡 Stop and Think

Consider a time in your own educational career when you received constructive feedback that was particularly helpful. From whom did you receive this feedback, and what made it so resonant? Did the deliverer highlight your strengths and areas for growth, or seem to intuit your end goal, perhaps even better than you could articulate at the time? What tone or technique did they use? Next, call to mind a time when you received feedback that felt unhelpful or that you had a harder time receiving. What factors led to that less ideal experience?

As you reflect, try to identify the qualities of effective and ineffective feedback and consider how you apply those qualities in your own responses to students. As you experiment with AI, do you see it incorporating those same qualities? Can you prompt it to do so? How can you take the results of your reflection and use them to hone your prompting of AI tools, ensuring a more impactful feedback experience for yourself and your students?

Developing and Honing Critical Literacy

We've discussed in prior chapters and know inherently the many possible harms of AI technologies. In the ELA classroom, plagiarism, deepfakes, the perpetuation of misinformation through hallucinations, and misleading or exploitative digital content are all of immediate concern. Teaching critical literacy has always been central to the discipline—teaching students about proper citations, quotations, and fair use; about the difference between summary and analysis; about digital citizenship and the validation of one's sources (especially secondary sources); about leading with inquiry rather than trusting what a text claims as true; about developing original arguments that appeal to readers' emotions, sense of logic, and ethics, and that move beyond conjecture and opinion to portray rigorous research. All of these skills have long defined the work of the literacy classroom.

But now we have an added challenge. We need to teach the importance of integrity in an era when AI-generated text is often imperceptible while also teaching students to discern the validity of the content they consume. The former requires SEL competencies (responsible decision-making, self-management), and the latter, cultural competence (analyses of bias, misrepresentation, monolithic viewpoints, etc.).

Here are several ways to begin:

1. **The Triangle Test.** "In academic research, scholars rely on the 'triangulation of data,' or, in qualitative research, 'a strategy to test validity through the convergence of information from different sources to ensure that their information is reliable and integritous" (Collins, 2024b, p. 1; Carter et al., 2014, p. 545). I recently wrote in a blog post for teachers through Write the World:

    > Inspired by triangulation, encourage students to seek out three sources that support an AI response, to showcase their due diligence in checking for hallucinations or, in the case of audiovisual information, deepfakes. Can they verify the validity of this information across different types of sources—for example, primary and secondary, or print and audio or visual? How might they assess the validity of these additional sources, such as by checking school library databases, speaking with a local librarian, or verifying source claims? Invite them to write a reflective memo regarding their

process, how they verified these three cross-checked sources, and how their thinking changed (about the topic and the research process) across time.

(Collins, 2024b, p. 1)

2. **Peer Educators.** We believe in taking a democratic approach to classroom environments and engaging youth in conversations about practices and policies that impact them. Thus, rather than setting AI regulations for students, consider engaging them in critical discourse about their views on AI and the reasons why they hold those views. After discussing their perspectives on the pros and cons of this technology, position them as youth leaders in your learning community tasked with educating younger students about ethical, responsible AI usage.

Such an assignment might invoke writings aligned with Common Core State Standards for informational writing; for example, students can create informational flyers, news articles, or multimedia presentations to share with students in a peer classroom, such as an ELA class a grade or two below their own. How can students conduct credible research and distill pertinent information in an accessible way for a younger audience? What do they know about their intended audience, and how might that information impact the form and content of their final product? Does their positioning on AI change when they're communicating with a younger audience—and why or why not? How might they learn about, and pass along knowledge of, the equity implications of AI?

Whether a lesson, unit, or semester-long role, this activity cultivates social-emotional skills inherent in mentoring, requiring students to engage with AI-related materials through a new vantage point while reflecting on their own ethics, morals, and learning. It's similar to how some schools enlist older students to teach younger students about climate change and recycling, perhaps embarking together on a community service project; here, too, in the context of AI, students can practice social-emotional and leadership skills while building meaningful relationships across grade levels (or even schools, in the case of elementary–high school pairings).

3. **Deepfake Ekphrasis.** Inspire students to get creative in their efforts to educate others about AI by introducing them to new forms of writing, such as ekphrastic poetry. After learning about deepfakes, for example, students might utilize multimedia AI technology to create an (innocuous) deepfake of their own or find an (appropriate) deepfake online to use as the visual inspiration for a poem. Ekphrastic poetry is poetry that is written in response to a work of art—a photograph, painting, collage. Often, the poem narrates the artwork in some way, such as from the perspective of an object pictured. The form encourages students' comparative analyses of multiple art forms, critical thinking about juxtaposition, and—that old refrain–intended audience.

   To extend their roles as responsible AI youth educators, students might create ekphrastic poems in response to cartoon deepfakes that call attention, in poetic form, to the potential perils of misinformation, then bind their ekphrases into a chapbook or children's book to share with a younger class. Or you might facilitate a gallery walk in a school hallway or auditorium, in which students' ekphrases and, optionally, reflective writers' statements similarly raise awareness and concern over the powers of AI technologies for inappropriate persuasion, propaganda creation, and/or perpetuation of inequitable or defamatory media content. Of course, you'll need to tailor this assignment to your context and objectives and structure it carefully to stay within appropriate guardrails, but when students have opportunities to practice informative and creative writing in tandem, through multimedia engagement, their investment in the learning task often expands.

4. **Prioritizing Primary Sources.** As important as it is to teach students how to discern whether research conducted using AI tools is valid, reliable, and unbiased, so is it helpful to center primary sources in their learning—first, as a means of checking the integrity of secondary sources and AI responses, and second, as a means of moving beyond AI to ensure that, though a powerful addition to research, it doesn't supplant the potency of these sources.

To engage in research processes in a more intimate way, encourage students to study primary sources at local museums, libraries, or through digital collections, to support their analytical, informational, or creative writing projects (the latter presents a great opportunity to talk about the rigorous research often involved in teens' favorite genres, like science fiction or historical fiction, which sometimes comes as a surprise to them).

Next, invite them to create primary sources of their own and/or to collect original data; teach them about and invite them to practice, for example, interview techniques with which to collect oral histories or to source quotes for a journalism project. They might use AI tools to simulate an interviewee, through writing or speaking, as they get the hang of sitting in the interviewer's chair—before moving into the "field" to interview real-world subjects they've identified.

Box 4.4 ♀ Stop and Think

Consider a time when you believed misinformation—whether falling for a scam email, a Photoshopped magazine image, a rumor, or a political news article that wasn't adequately fact-checked. We are all vulnerable to believing—even if only for a few minutes—the surface-level information conveyed in the media that pervade our lives.

It's important to normalize that susceptibility, especially with students, to avoid stigma. With young people, share a personal anecdote or two about your own experiences and the action-steps you took to dig deeper and debunk your initial misconceptions. Doing so normalizes and models critical literacy practices and highlights that no one is "immune" from needing to do this work and educate others.

Bringing Characters to Life

For the first time, we have the tools to make literary characters, authors, activists, and historical figures more vivid in students' minds through AI simulations. With this opportunity comes, first, the responsibility to think together with learners about how to assess historical and cultural accuracy before we introduce AI simulation activities in which students may be vulnerable to believing that AI-generated figures represent the real (rather than statistically calculated) words, looks, or beliefs of those whom they portray.

To begin, ask students what questions they might pose to themselves to determine the accuracy of an AI-simulated figure. Some sample questions might include the following:

- *What tone, dialect, or voice does the AI portray? What sources—such as letters, speeches, or video clips—can I consult to compare and contrast this voice with that of the actual figure/character?*
- *What do I know about this figure's identity, positionality, and perspective? How do I know this information? Do I see this information reflected in AI responses?*

♦ What biases or stereotypes might be portrayed in this AI simulation? How do I know, and how can I counteract them in my work?
♦ What is the purpose of this simulation? How might I use it as a starting place—deepening and extending my research by consulting other sources?

Once you've established some ground rules for critical analysis and responsible engagement, consider leveraging AI simulations of protagonists, poets, or changemakers through the following activities.

Box 4.5 AI Simulation Activities to Promote SEL and Cultural Responsiveness in ELA

Activity #1: Interview Inquiry. In the way that you might invite students to practice their interviewing skills with an AI interviewee before entering the field for a journalism project, noted before, so might you invite students to plan for and conduct interviews with AI simulations of characters, celebrities, authors, or activists. Planning open-ended interview questions for these figures requires students to exercise social-emotional skills (self- and social awareness, self-management, responsible decision-making, etc.) as well as cultural competence, particularly if interviewing across ages, races, socioeconomic statuses, time periods, and more.

Students might write an analytical paper about a protagonist's motivations and intentions, then engage in a simulated AI interview with that character and compare and contrast whether their initial thesis statement still feels accurate (recognizing, of course, that AI is not the benefactor of truth, may not accurately portray the character, and should supplement students' analytical engagement with the literary text itself). Or they might chat with civil rights leaders of the past, who participated in racial or disability movements, as an exit ticket activity that launches them into homework assignments in which they engage with primary source archival documents from those movements or listen to real audio clips of those leaders speaking, then compare/contrast the validity of the AI chat based on what they learn from source material (note that, because AI is trained primarily on publicly accessible content on the Internet, it may struggle to represent historical figures who are lesser known and/or minoritized). Or perhaps a student writes an imitation poem inspired by a figure like Maya Angelou, then solicits "peer review" feedback from a simulated Angelou herself (again questioning and analyzing the cultural and historical accuracy of the experience).

The purpose of simulated interviews can vary across assignment contexts, with the intention being to open new doors for engagement—albeit requiring significant disclaimers and a discerning eye about the nonrepresentative nature of the digital interactions, though that caveat can itself cultivate students' critical analysis capabilities.

Activity #2: Comparative Characters. Building upon the digital interview activity, students might conduct analytical writing in which they compare and contrast a character's portrayal in a literary work and that character's portrayal by AI. What similarities and differences do students notice between the original literary rendition and the facsimile in their chatbox? What questions does the simulated character convincingly answer, and where are there significant discrepancies that give away authenticity? How do students think differently about the literary work after engaging in such a simulation? These exercises and conversations can again support students' analytical thinking and engagement with texts while simultaneously supporting their critical literacy skills.

Activity #3: AI Elegy. In February 2024, artist Justin Sims created the series, "Give Them Flowers," a tribute to Black changemakers like Muhammad Ali, Malcolm X, Bob Marley, Aaliyah, Kobe Bryant, and more. In the series, AI-generated video renditions show these figures peacefully roaming vibrant flower fields—an homage to their nonviolent leadership and a sharp contrast to the brutality that they faced in a racist culture. The footage is moving, and it showcases a new way to use AI—to bring to simulated life those who have passed, to pay tribute to their legacies.

To that end, students may create, perhaps as an accompaniment to a lesson on elegy poems in an ELA context, AI-generated images or videos to accompany their own elegiac verses or prose. They might first engage in an AI simulation in which they chat with the AI rendition of the figure whom they're elegizing. Doing so invites into the ELA classroom multimedia narrative activities, facilitates conversations about archival practices, and allows for multiple modes of representation, expression, and engagement—the tenets of the Universal Design for Learning framework that enhances accessibility in the classroom (CAST, 2024a).

Facilitating Multimodal Instruction to Meet Diverse Learning Needs

Through an equity lens, we've considered those whom AI technologies exclude—those whose voices and identities are marginalized or misrepresented in generative artificial intelligence output; those who lack access to these emerging technological tools; those whose jobs may be in peril due to AI replacement, particularly jobs that rely on procedural tasks.

Simultaneously, we would be wise to consider whether and how AI technologies can enhance inclusion in unprecedented ways; for whom, and through what uses, can generative AI tools open doors previously closed?

Universal Design for Learning (UDL), mentioned previously, is a research-backed accessibility framework created by Anne Meyer, David H. Rose, and David Gordon, founders of the educational not-for-profit CAST; its guidelines

> . . . are not meant to be a "prescription" or a "checklist," but a tool that offers a set of suggestions that can be applied to reduce barriers, sustain and honor learners' multiple identities, and maximize learning opportunities for every learner. The Guidelines can be mixed and

matched according to specific learning goals and can be applied to particular content areas and contexts.

(CAST, 2024a, p. 1)

The framework is elegant and nuanced, founded on extensive neuropsychological research regarding how the brain learns; particularly, Meyer et al. (2014) consider the three major brain networks involved in the learning process:

> "**Affective networks (sic)** that monitor the internal and external environment to set priorities, to motivate, and to engage learning and behavior.
> **Recognition networks (sic)** that sense and perceive information in the environment and transform it into usable knowledge.
> **Strategic networks (sic)** that plan, organize, and initiate purposeful actions in the environment."
>
> (p. 54)

Those who've taken educational psychology or child development courses en route to becoming educators may recognize these networks as related to the work of psychologist Lev Vygotsky, who similarly "described three prerequisites for learning: Engagement with the learning task; Recognition of the information to be learned; and Strategies to process that information" (Meyer et al., 2014, p. 55). From these "major three" come the three organizing principles of UDL—that accessible teaching and learning involves multiple modes of *engagement* with learning tasks, *representation* of content, and *action and expression* of learning. From there, the framework emphasizes access, support, and executive functioning, highlighting principles teachers may keep in mind during the design of learning environments, experiences, and collateral.

Set against these principles, AI may be a tool for enhancing accessibility through UDL, allowing for the following:

- **Multiple Means of Engagement.** This first tenet encompasses student autonomy, belonging, and SEL competencies like self- and social awareness, among others (CAST, 2024b, p. 1). Using the AI tools and activities mentioned throughout this text targets these skills. Offering students the option to employ AI tools as aids in the learning process further provides them with agency over their learning, enhancing metacognitive awareness of their cognitive processes and intentionality in their academic engagement.
- **Multiple Means of Representation.** As an educator, you may now instantaneously translate curricular content into multimedia formats such as images, videos, graphs, charts, or graphic organizers, in addition to text, thus creating multiple representations of the same content, and in a way that is customizable pursuant to the needs and preferences of each learner. Students, of course, may also have this freedom in the creation of their own work, representing their learning through multiple formats. Additionally, simulation activities allow students to emulate real-world contexts, reinforcing the transfer and application of knowledge, itself an executive functioning tenet of this overarching UDL principle (CAST, 2024b, p. 1).
- **Multiple Means of Action and Expression.** This tenet comprises guidance like "Optimize access to accessible materials and assistive and accessible technologies and tools . . . Build fluencies with graduated support . . . Address biases related to modes of expression and communication . . . [and] Challenge exclusionary practices" (CAST, 2024b, p. 1), among others. Using AI tools, you can strive to fulfill these objectives by creating adaptive learning tasks that adjust levels of challenge to learners' performance, facilitating analytical activities regarding the biases inherent in AI-generated content, and again

promoting inclusion by acknowledging and discussing the exclusionary components of AI and enhancing equity through the production (and students' production) of flexible, multiform content.

The adaptability and multimodality of AI-generated content, particularly when aligned with UDL principles, may position educators to better serve students with a range of learning disabilities. Imagine, for instance, the rapidity with which we can now create, for students with language-based learning challenges, AI-generated sentence-frame worksheets, essay outline charts, and/or text-to-audio content to scaffold composition. Or, for students who struggle with executive functioning, the ability to now co-create goal charts, calendars, schedules, visual maps of a project plan, reminder notes, and more. And for students who are English language learners, who may also benefit from multimodal content, we can now more easily offer customized vocabulary sets; images and video content to accompany new words or difficult narratives, translation flashcards; and content tailored to varying Lexile levels, such as four levels of the same short story. These students, too, may use AI translation, grammar, and mechanics tools; chat activities that allow for greater time-on-task during written and vocal language practice; and simulations that facilitate language practice and confidence-building in advance of in-person discourse (Ferlazzo, 2024; Huynh, 2023).

Across use cases, in addition to speed and customizability, AI tools can enhance student-centered pedagogies when teachers align generated collateral with students' backgrounds and interests. For example, you might create three vocabulary sets at the same Lexile level but tailored to students' extracurricular activities. Whereas it would have previously taken excess time to create individualized content, we may now leverage our knowledge of students as whole people to support their motivation and, requisitely, performance.

Enhancing College and Career Readiness

Postsecondary and professional preparation remain pertinent equity and access issues across American school systems. School counselors, typically leaders in students' college and career preparations, are often overburdened with an unmanageable caseload; for instance, "Although [the American School Counselor Association] recommends a 250-to-1 ratio of students to school counselors, the national average is actually 385-to-1 for the 2022–2023 school year (the most recent year for which data is available)" (ASCA, 2024, p. 1). In the midst of a national youth mental health crisis, the impacts of which often also unfurl in the offices of school counselors, these professionals are all the more strained; in 2023, reports claimed that U.S. schools were "100,000 mental health staff short" (St. George, 2023, p. 1).

This means neither students' college and/or career readiness nor mental health needs are wholly supported.

ELA teachers often pick up some of the overflow with regard to college and career readiness, supporting students' college application essays or looking over their draft résumés, for example. Might AI support this work, perhaps by allowing for differentiated station rotation activities (Tucker, 2021) in which some students engage with AI activities that support their applying to college or preparing for their future careers, while teachers provide more hands-on support to students?

AI-rotation activities in the ELA context might include the following:

1. **Interview and Negotiation Simulations.** Students can search for job postings that align with careers they might be interested in pursuing after school, enter a posting into a tool like ChatGPT, and prompt the AI to engage

in a back-and-forth pseudo-interview as if they were the hiring manager; or, a student preparing to apply to college might prompt the AI to respond to them as an admissions officer from each of their top five colleges, engaging in pseudo-interviews and comparing and contrasting the subtle differences that they notice. This simulation acquaints students with the types of questions they might expect during in-person interviews and, critically, creates space for them to practice the skill of designing questions to pose to interviewers. Students can include in their initial prompt an instruction for the AI tool to provide feedback on their performance when asking; they can also focus that feedback, telling the AI:

- *When I ask for it, please share constructive criticism on how aligned my questions to you as the interviewer were with the goals and mission of the University.*
- *When I prompt you to, please share constructive criticism on how I can make my answers more convincing and/or succinct.*
- *At the conclusion of our mock interview, please share a detailed analysis of which questions I was strongest at answering, which I need to improve upon, and how I might go about making those improvements.*

The same activity suits a negotiation context as well, offering students a chance to practice requesting and negotiating a salary or designated benefits, acquainting them with these real-world professional interactions, particularly in contexts where teacher-student ratios prevent meaningful mock interview programs at school.

2. **Tailored Résumé and Cover Letter Feedback.** As in the previous example, students might share with ChatGPT a job description and ask for Socratic feedback on application materials. Career and technical education teacher Michelle Lockhart writes in her *Edutopia* article,

"Teaching CTE Students About Work-Related Uses of AI," that

> for cover letters, an AI-as-tutor prompt might look like this: "Can you develop questions to help me draft a cover letter based on this job description?" Students should input the job description for a position they're interested in applying for. The AI will provide a series of questions to help the student develop a cover letter. To further personalize a résumé to a specific job, students can prompt the AI to help them develop phrases for their résumé. Once students incorporate the phrases into their résumé, they can then put the text from their résumé back into the AI platform and ask it to provide feedback.
>
> (2024, p. 1)

3. **Digital College and Career Coach.** Many of us are familiar with the multiple-choice tests once used to support students' determining what fields they might like to pursue after high school. In my own experience, they felt impersonal and, often, inaccurate. As a prerequisite to meaningful conversations with trusted mentors, coaches, and counselors, students might now opt to engage in discourse with an AI tool prompted to pose open-ended questions that guide students toward a clearer picture of their hopes and dreams for their professional lives. Students might then take the transcripts of these chats and/or a reflective memo that they write about their experience engaging with the tool in this way to ELA teachers or school counselors for more relational conversations about those goals.

4. **Mock Meet-Ups With Professionals Across Fields.** A fourth simulation activity invites students to prompt AI to respond from the perspective of a particular

professional, such as a contractor, lawyer, anthropologist, conservationist, or chef. You can also set up AI stations with predetermined prompts. Invite students to ask about the daily experience of this professional, their path to attaining the role, advice for young aspirants, what they can do in high school to better position themselves to pursue this path, etc. Of course, it's ideal to also pair students with mentors in the real world through shadowing opportunities; class visits from individuals across careers; and/or internships, volunteering opportunities, and more (and, in these scenarios, a mock conversation with a professional via AI might prepare students to better liaise with and ask meaningful questions of these experts). But amid the constraints of many classrooms, such community connections don't always manifest, and so this type of interaction might offer a middle ground without forsaking real-world immersion and connection as the central goal.

Relating back to SEL, these college and career preparation activities may support students' sense of future, a term used to describe one's ability to imagine, dream, and positively plan for the life that one desires; importantly, individuals with a history of trauma can have an attenuated ability to engage in such thinking, experiencing what psychologists call a "foreshortened sense of future," or the "feeling as if life will be cut short without any real explanation as to why" (Tull, 2024, p. 1). Such a phenomenon requires the support of trained mental health professionals, but I share it here, not only because it connects to social-emotional learning, but because it augments the importance of supporting students as they orient themselves toward the future. It is pertinent that we utilize all tools at our disposal to ensure that students feel bolstered by our presence and instruction as they work to envision, not only their future, but the collective future that they desire to make manifest.

Creative Writing

Many of the practices named before and throughout this book apply to creative and expressive writing instruction in the ELA classroom, such as students' utilization of AI tools to (a) solicit feedback during workshops; (b) check grammar and mechanics; (c) translate phrases from their language of origin to that of their academic essay; (d) generate model texts; (e) emulate an admired author with whom to brainstorm; (f) create a backward-planned calendar with which to track writing progress; or (g) produce multimedia content to complement one's original story, poem, or narrative. During creative writing, students might also apply some of the activities we explored in the SEL chapter, such as those that promote internal self-awareness. After identifying an area for growth in a given genre of writing, for example, they might then use AI to help themselves improve; if a student names scansion or rhyme scheme as a skill they would like to strengthen when writing poetry, they might ask ChatGPT to help them generate a list of rhyming words pursuant to a particular theme, mood, topic, or image, from which they can select the most salient for their verse; or, after soliciting feedback about their scansion, ask for a list of words with a certain number of stressed or unstressed syllables with which to experiment as they refine and revise, say, a sonnet written in iambic pentameter.

To practice, we invite you to use any or all of the beautiful poems penned by Jordan Stempleman, which appear as poetic reflections throughout this text. With any of these poems, you might begin with a student- or instructor-led Socratic discussion using questions like these:

- *What is the central message of this poem, and how do you know?*
- *How is the theme of communication present in this poem? What lines particularly demonstrate this theme?*

- *What allusions to technology and/or innovation do you notice in this verse? Where in the text do you notice these, and what impact do they have on the message, voice, or mood of the verse?*
- *How does this poem relate, explicitly or implicitly, to artificial intelligence? Get creative as you make connections between this verse and our modern moment.*
- *What poetic techniques do you notice Stempleman using in this work? What impact do those techniques have on you as a reader?*
- *What does this poem inspire you to consider, question, or remember, and why?*
- *What central tensions or conflicts are at the heart of this poem, and how do you know?*

Invite students to select one poem to emulate as they create an "imitation poem." This might mean that they

- Borrow the poem's title and write a new verse inspired by it.
- Create a "found poem" using words and phrases that they see in media, news articles, literature, ads, social media posts, and/or other poems, amalgamating them into a poem that, through careful juxtaposition, shares a similar message to that of Stempleman's (remember to ask them to cite their sources for each line borrowed/found).
- Write a poem to or about AI that engages communication-related themes similar to those that they identify in Stempleman's verse.
- Write a poem in response to Stempleman's poem, engaging in antiphonal, or call-and-response, poetry. Before engaging in this activity, work with students to explore the history of antiphonal technique, which has rich roots in Black and Indigenous oratorical cultures; conduct research together to contextualize this artform and to

introduce or discuss the notion of cultural appropriation, considering together whether/how this form has been appropriated across time and how students can acknowledge its history in their work.
- Write a series of poems in response to a theme, image, speaker, or event that they identify in one of Stempleman's poems. Each poem in the series should take a different form, such as free verse, haiku, and sonnet, or pantoum, tanka, and villanelle. Invite students to research the cultural traditions backing their chosen poetic forms.

No matter which activity you and your students select, invite them to use AI in the ways noted before, to generate new ideas regarding diction, syntax, and structure, and/or to solicit one type of feedback, among many, during their iteration and revision.

We've explored a wide range of possibilities for integrating AI into ELA in ways that support students' social-emotional learning and cultural responsiveness. The following are the key takeaways.

Box 4.6 AI Usage and Benefits When Teaching ELA

- Use AI tools to simulate students' intended audiences, supporting their brainstorming, drafting, and revision processes in writing.
- Scaffold and supplement peer and instructor review with AI-generated feedback.
- Support students' critical thinking and research skills.
- Enhance multimodal instruction and Universal Design for Learning through the AI-assisted generation of multimedia content and collateral, enhancing accessibility.
- Augment students' college and career readiness through AI simulation activities.

♦ Support students' creative writing skills by using AI as a tool in the writing process and by infusing themes related to technology and communication into the content of creative writing assignments.

Box 4.7 Try Out the Tech and Reflect

Consider a challenging professional situation that you have encountered or anticipate encountering in your own life, related to the examples provided. Perhaps it's requesting a raise, giving or receiving a quarterly review, or revamping your résumé for a new educational leadership position. What thoughts and feelings first surface for you when you think about this task? Are you eager to tackle it, or are you avoiding it? What, specifically, feels most promising and most daunting about it, and why?

Try out an AI simulation yourself, casting the bot as manager, supervisee, recruiter, principal, or another relevant persona. See how your prompting can best frame the relevant personality, voice, and tone, then engage in the simulation exercise to get a feel for the student experience before facilitating similar activities in your classroom. What feels most and least helpful, and why? Do you garner different results across AI tools, such as from ChatGPT and Gemini? What can you learn about AI from this firsthand experience, and how might those learnings inform your work with students?

References

Alleyne, C. (2024, July 26). One teen's perspective on writing with AI. *Write the World Blog.* https://blog.writetheworld.org/one-teens-perspective-on-writing-with-ai

ASCA. (2024). School counselor roles & ratios. *School Counselor Roles & Ratios—American School Counselor Association (ASCA)*. www.schoolcounselor.org/About-School-Counseling/School-Counselor-Roles-Ratios

Carter, N., Bryant-Lukosius, D., DiCenso, A., Blythe, J., & Neville, A. J. (2014). The use of triangulation in qualitative research. *Oncology Nursing Forum, 41*(5), 545–547. https://doi.org/10.1188/14.onf.545-547

CAST, Inc. (2024a). *About the Graphic Organizer|UDL Guidelines*. https://udlguidelines.cast.org/more/about-graphic-organizer/

CAST, Inc. (2024b). *The UDL Guidelines*. https://udlguidelines.cast.org/

Cherry, K. (2023, April 4). How the theory of mind helps us understand others. *Verywell Mind*. www.verywellmind.com/theory-of-mind-4176826

Collins, B. (2024a, May 10). Teaching the writing process. *Write the World Blog*. https://blog.writetheworld.org/teaching-the-writing-process

Collins, B. (2024b, September 9). Teaching critical literacy in the age of AI. *Write the World Blog*. https://blog.writetheworld.org/teaching-critical-literacy-in-the-age-of-a.i

Common Core State Standards Initiative. (2024). English language arts standards. *Common Core State Standards Initiative*. https://www.thecorestandards.org/ELA-Literacy/

Ferlazzo, L. (2024, March 22). How to use AI tools to support English-language learners (opinion). *Education Week*. www.edweek.org/teaching-learning/opinion-how-to-use-ai-tools-to-support-english-language-learners/2024/03

Gottschall, J. (2013). *The storytelling animal: How stories make us human*. Mariner Books, an imprint of HarperCollins Publishers.

Huynh, T. (2023, November 21). Using AI to support multilingual students. *Edutopia*. www.edutopia.org/article/using-ai-support-multilingual-students/

Lockhart, M. (2024, March 15). Teaching CTE students about work-related uses of AI. *Edutopia*. www.edutopia.org/article/teaching-cte-students-use-ai/

Meyer, A., Rose, D., & Gordon, D. (2014). *Universal Design for Learning: Theory and practice*. CAST Professional Publishing.

Nakkula, M. J., & Toshalis, E. (2020). *Understanding youth adolescent development for educators*. Harvard Education Press.

National Association of Educational Progress. (2012). The nation's report card: Writing 2011. *Executive Summary*. https://nces.ed.gov/nationsreportcard/pubs/main2011/2012470.aspx

Picou, A. (2023, December 4). Are schools making writing a priority? *The Learning Agency Lab*. https://the-learning-agency-lab.com/the-learning-curve/are-schools-making-writing-a-priority

Schaffhauser, D. (2020, August 25). Research: Students need to spend more time writing. *Technological Horizons in Education*. https://thejournal.com/articles/2020/08/25/students-need-to-spend-more-time-writing.aspx

Sommers, N. I. (2013). *Responding to student writers*. Bedford/St. Martin's.

St. George, D. (2023, August 31). In a crisis, schools are 100,000 mental health staff short. *The Washington Post*. www.washingtonpost.com/education/2023/08/31/mental-health-crisis-students-have-third-therapists-they-need/

Tucker, C. (2021, October 29). The station rotation model: Prioritize differentiation, student agency & 4Cs of 21st-century learning. *Dr. Catlin Tucker*. https://catlintucker.com/2021/10/station-rotation-model/

Tull, M. (2024, July 21). How to cope with a sense of foreshortened future. *Verywell Mind*. www.verywellmind.com/coping-with-a-foreshortened-future-ptsd-2797225

Zak, P. J. (2012). *The moral molecule: The source of love and prosperity*. Dutton.

Poetic Reflection

Wait Here

Jordan Stempleman

there is an audible
rhythm a density
to a person

a limitless hand
windows &
afternoons a readiness

that rides of you
defines you
by your gamble or fifty-three

levels but internally
as autonomy
the lances of friends

the goodbye the I recall
the uncured noon
want times

of sharp contrast
alert colors from
computer from eyes

or turning little job time
to commonplace smiles
& care feel

if you
didn't write good
then I

didn't write good either
& the people
with you glow

the higher glow
in meanings so clear
embroiled

& primarily but them
a quasi-porous merge
of some original

health that so melts me
as a kind of freedom
a reminder silent really

like a poem
out of conceived
partial [insert]

diastolic amnesia
of too many resonances
& we to be

as something
as we are brief
mutual & in circulation

crumpling through
the we can do
zero & blue

ridden & written off
when all mouthed
of some convenience

each morning sound
a bellwether you know
the hour of forest

crowded by dunes
faced in a good way
by inwardness

the now within the
think I shouldn't so
the language roaming

roaming as the force
of radiations
plus

refusals something
the top quark used
to refuel

the idea of
identity our earthly
makes & modes

the whiz bang
we put forward once
the silence starts

the float of norms
of nothing now
we thin the thing

we thin the thing
so good
& so out of range

that the fires grow lost
in themselves
nothing more

than the care swept
away together
without the guide

to guide us
you hear that
right & nothing more

5
Enhancing Equitable History Instruction Through AI

Marlee S. Bunch

In 1960, amidst social division and racism, a group of students came together to collectively work toward equal rights and justice. This group included people such as John Lewis, Diane Nash, Charles Cobb, Bob Moses, and *many* others. What emerged from lunch counter sit-ins and protests grew into a student movement that helped to work toward voting rights, civil rights, equitable education, and so on. When I think about equitable history, I immediately think of the efforts and historical importance of the Student Non-Violent Coordinating Committee (SNCC, pronounced "Snick"), as they represented and stood for so many of the attributes we want to see in our classrooms today—collective effort, community involvement, student voices, and so forth. This is the history that students and classrooms need knowledge of, and this is the history that will help us create and sustain culturally responsive classrooms.

Unfortunately, my students' knowledge about history is typically limited to primarily Eurocentric history they have been taught in their schooling. Their knowledge of their own history and that of other cultures and groups seems minimal at best. The gaps they have are generally related to Black, Indigenous, Asian American and Pacific Islander, and Latina/o, history, as well as the history of other underrepresented groups, demonstrating the continued need to help our students discover and learn about history that is often overlooked. Research shows that learning about equitable history benefits everyone (Yilmaz, 2008, p. 40). Now more than ever, it is important that equitable and inclusive histories and stories are taught in our classrooms and interwoven in curricula. If we hope to foster empathy, respect, and perspective-taking, then our pedagogy and curricula must support and encourage understanding of both our country's vast history and the histories and experiences of various cultures and communities (local and global). Additionally, the perspectives we teach need to be researched, accurate, and inclusive. By marrying best practices for teaching history and social studies with AI tools, we can discover ways to expand and enhance student learning.

We have reviewed some of the concerns about AI in previous chapters, but for this chapter, let us shift our focus back to the potential positive aspects of AI and the ways that it can be coupled with good teaching practices to make content and curricula more engaging and creative. Again, consistently modeling for students the concerns and unreliable aspects of AI empowers them to better understand the power they have when they uniquely and humanly assess and analyze information. Stressing our human ability to connect, discuss, and reflect positions AI as a tool rather than a seemingly magical generator of information. History and social studies illuminate moments that can help students learn to appreciate, empathize with, and feel a full range of emotions as historical events are discussed. Here are a few tips to foster equitable and inclusive histories:

1. Expose students to stories not typically known (e.g., instead of teaching about Martin Luther King, Jr. or Rosa Parks,

who are widely known, teach about Medgar Evers, Dorie and Joyce Ladner, Vernon Dahmer, Grace Lee Boggs, and Yuri Kochiyama, among others). It is worth noting that AI will not be able to represent stories not typically known since it is trained on public Internet content, which is primarily Eurocentric. This means that unearthing and illuminating underrepresented stories and histories becomes even more important for the role of the educator.

2. Use history to explore issues of gender, race, culture, socioeconomics, identities, etc. History is an ideal way to help students explore their own positionality (lens) and intersectionality (the various aspects of who they are). Show relevance between the past and present.
3. Help dismantle mistruths, prejudices, and myths by looking at history in an honest manner and through varied perspectives and reliable sources.
4. Learn, unlearn, and relearn, challenging your students to do the same.
5. Use primary sources such as oral histories, photographs, and letters to show the human aspect of the people involved in historical movements.
6. Use the classroom as a place to build respect and connections with students, families, and the community.

Box 5.1 AI Usage and Benefits When Teaching History

- Use AI image generators (e.g., Canva) to give students a visual of historical moments.
- Use AI to help students access primary sources. For example, students can easily access historical documents, letters, and archival information using AI tools. AI can help students search through databases and identify relevant primary sources related to their topic (e.g., Transkribus, Digital Public Library of America).

- iCivics interactive simulations give an overview of topics such as voting, policies, governance, the legal system, etc. through gameplay and interactive elements.
- AI history chatbots (e.g., Hello History) can help students assess and analyze information and allow them to interact with historical figures. Inspecting information for accuracy is a great way to help students discern factual and inaccurate information.
- Use AI to expose students to art, cultures, and global appreciation and understanding of communities and people unlike their own.
- Use AI to allow students to plan presentations and/or practice speaking and listening.
- Use AI to help students brainstorm and write essay outlines for history assignments or research.

Let's See What AI Can Do

Spending time experimenting with AI tools is one of the best ways to begin understanding the tools and platforms and the ways in which you can utilize them in your learning space. Google's Gemini app was one I had not yet tried, so I spent time putting in various prompts to see what it would produce, its responses, and what information might be inaccurate or misleading for students. I told it that I needed a history lesson that was inclusive and equitable, and here is what it produced:

Inclusive History Lesson: The Civil Rights Movement

This lesson explores the Civil Rights Movement in the United States from a perspective that highlights the diversity of experience and contribution.

Learning Objectives:

- *Students will be able to identify key events and figures of the Civil Rights Movement.*
- *Students will be able to analyze the role of different groups (racial, ethnic, gender) within the movement.*
- *Students will be able to discuss the importance of nonviolent resistance.*

Activities:

1. *Brainstorming: Begin by asking students what they already know about the Civil Rights Movement. This activates prior knowledge and allows students to see how their understanding fits into the bigger picture.*
2. *Multiple Perspectives: Instead of focusing on a single narrative, present the movement through the lens of different groups.*
   - *Explore the role of prominent figures like Dr. Martin Luther King, Jr., Rosa Parks, Malcolm X, and Cesar Chavez, highlighting their unique approaches and contributions.*
   - *Discuss the experiences of everyday people who participated in boycotts, sit-ins, and freedom rides.*
   - *Consider the role of women in the movement, acknowledging figures like Claudette Colvin and Dorothy Height.*
3. *Primary Sources: Analyze primary sources like photographs, speeches, or music to gain a deeper understanding of the time period.*
   - *This could involve analyzing Dr. King's "I Have a Dream" speech, looking at photographs of the lunch counter sit-ins, or listening to freedom songs.*

4. *Discussion:* Facilitate a respectful discussion about the challenges and triumphs of the movement. Encourage students to consider the complexities and the ongoing pursuit of racial equality.

Remember:

- *Inclusive Language: Use inclusive language that avoids bias or stereotypes.*
- *Multiple Resources: Incorporate a variety of resources beyond traditional textbooks to represent diverse voices and perspectives.*
- *Open Dialogue: Create a safe space for open dialogue and critical thinking.*

Extension Activities:

- *Students can research a specific figure or event from the Civil Rights Movement and present their findings to the class.*
- *The class can create a timeline of the Civil Rights Movement, highlighting key events and figures from different backgrounds.*
- *Students can write a letter to their future selves reflecting on the importance of social justice movements and their own role in creating a more equitable society.*

By using these strategies, you can create a history lesson that is not only informative but also fosters empathy, understanding, and a commitment to a more just future.

(GoogleAI, 2024)

Now, let us take a moment to walk through the lesson and assess its strengths and weaknesses, which is something you would want to do prior to implementing any lesson that you did not create. The lesson is broad, like many of AI's initial responses. It does not identify dates, define key terms (e.g., nonviolent resistance), or make any mention of why the Civil Rights Movement occurred. It lacks the details of discussing or mentioning Jim Crow, segregation, racism, lack of access to voting rights/education, the Civil Rights Act and/or Voting Act that emerged due to civil rights advocacy, and so forth. This lesson would require the teacher to build in background information, context, and connections. I appreciated that it mentioned key figures not typically discussed (e.g., Malcom X and Cesar Chavez, Claudette Colvin and Dorothy Height), but it also failed to mention some important key figures of the movement (e.g., Julian Bond, Ella Baker, Fannie Lou Hamer, and many others). Additionally, the lesson fails to make any mention of coalitions, student contributions to the movement, or the fact that efforts were grassroots and community-based. This lesson did not fully address the prompt that I provided, which was a lesson that was inclusive and equitable. So, how can we make it better, and what aspects do we need to reflect on? If we pause and reflect on how this lesson could be improved, we might consider the following:

1. How does the lesson allow for differentiation?
2. What details, specifics, context, or background information is lacking or missing? How can you (the educator) fill in those gaps to make the lesson robust?
3. What might we want to unlearn or relearn about the topic at hand, and how will this support our teaching of the topic?
4. Whose histories or stories might the AI lesson or activity overlook? How can we make the lesson more robust with more perspectives and voices, specifically underrepresented voices?
5. How can we improve the lesson? What resources should we include? What primary or secondary sources should we reference? How can we triangulate the content by using multiple data sources?
6. What connections to the present day could we build into the lesson so that students see connections to their own lives or global narratives?

Relying on AI lessons alone is simply not enough. Think of it rather as a space to collaborate, research, use your expertise, and vet information before introducing an AI lesson to your students. This will help to ensure that the content you are sharing with students is accurate, well researched and culturally responsive. Analyzing lessons also asks us to consider the texts we utilize or that AI might reference. When considering texts, it is important to think about the following questions:

- Do the texts and reading material in the lesson avoid stereotypes, saviorism, tropes, and cultural appropriation?
- Does the text encourage analysis?
- Does the text lend itself to varied learning modalities?
- Are the setting, themes, and characters in the text inclusive, diverse, and accurately represented?
- Does the text acknowledge truthful historical information?
- How does the story help dismantle stereotypes, tropes, and myths that negatively impact people or groups?
- Can you use the un/HUSH framework to include materials that increase cultural responsiveness?

Effective Methods for Teaching Social Studies/History

AI can be useful in helping to bring history and social studies topics and curricula to life, making them relevant. AI tools can help build engagement and help students connect the past to the present—an important way to help students make connections and notice historical patterns. Inquiry-based learning strategies are paramount when thinking about social studies and history curricula, as is culturally responsive pedagogy. AI can help supplement and enhance these skills in the following ways (Llego, 2023):

1. **Research Assistance.** Analysis tools and search engines that help students find and organize relevant information regarding a topic they are researching.

2. **Feedback Tools.** These tools offer students immediate feedback.
3. **Access.** Access to primary sources and digital archives.

Let's say, for example, that you are designing a lesson around historical coalitions. You could explore many people and/or groups, but for the sake of this lesson, let's say you are planning to offer students a choice between the following groups:

- The Rainbow Coalition (Chicago)
- Asian American Political Alliance (AAPA)
- The Black Panther Party
- Student Non-Violent Coordinating Committee (SNCC) and the volunteers of Freedom Summer

Students would first need to establish a general context and background about each group and person. This is an ideal place to utilize AI research assistance (this would be done in conjunction with the library, peer-reviewed articles, primary sources, books, etc.). Next, students could draft writing related to their topic (whatever assignment is given)—here is where AI feedback tools will be useful. Finally, ask students to choose 2–3 primary sources to support their learning. This might be listening to an oral history, analyzing a photograph, or examining a document. This is important as it helps them determine if the information AI is providing is accurate through triangulation and the verification of facts.

Through using the various tools mentioned before, educators can help reinforce and expand critical thinking, analysis, and inquiry-based learning. History and social studies are exciting subjects, as they allow educators to introduce students to the importance of stories, traditions, and global awareness. Students can have opportunities to share stories, recognize shared experiences, and honor oral storytelling throughout various cultures. Making sense of the world today requires that students understand the past. AI can help you make history more accessible for students. AI is merely an entry point, but good teaching and curricula are what will help students effectively practice and apply critical skills that they will use throughout their lives.

> **Box 5.2 Try Out the Tech and Reflect**

Take a moment to visit MagicSchool or ChatGPT to generate a lesson plan or activity related to social studies or history. Consider the following questions once you find one that you are interested in:

1. How can I enhance this lesson or activity with inclusive texts?
2. Where does the lesson or activity fall short? What are its benefits?
3. Choose one time period in history that you know well. Ask AI about that time period and then assess and evaluate its responses. What do you notice?

References

GoogleAI. (2024). *Gemini*. (January 20 version) [Large language model]. https://gemini.google.com

Llego, M. A. (2023, March 22). Adapting to AI in education: Strategies for encouraging critical thinking and human connection in the classroom. *TeacherPH*. www.teacherph.com/adapting-ai-education-strategies-critical-thinking-human-connection/#google_vignette

Yilmaz, K. (2008). A vision of history teaching and learning: Thoughts on history education in secondary schools. *The High School Journal, 92*(2), 37–46. www.jstor.org/stable/40660807

Epilogue

Looking Ahead

Marlee S. Bunch and Brittany R. Collins

As we look toward the future, we will undoubtedly encounter many changes in education and our world. There will be advancements, setbacks, and unforeseen innovations that influence how we teach and how we and our students learn. We don't need to tell you that, in our current moment, educators are facing myriad obstacles, personal and systemic. Inequities have impacted our educational system for far too long.

Despite the historical and current hurdles we face in education, we encourage teachers to maintain a sense of innovation, collaboration, and hopefulness. A recent AI education summit at Stanford University showed promise for the future as educators and researchers gathered to learn about the possibilities of AI in education. One of the big takeaways from the event was that "great teachers remain the cornerstone of effective learning," but "AI presents an opportunity to support teachers as they refine their craft at scale" (Price, 2024). This glimmer of hope centers AI's ability to help us tailor lessons to achieve individualized learning, shorten our planning time, spark creativity, and support our students' strengths and areas of need. These abilities make AI a worthwhile tool when used by mindful and professional educators who are attuned to the needs of all students.

Our classrooms are always evolving. In the 1950s, the overhead projector emerged on the scene. Though initially used during World War II for military briefings, it eventually made its way into classrooms. I imagine it was initially daunting, with its bright bulb and whirring noise, and the delicate transparent films that had to be positioned carefully so that all of the content was visible. In 1959, the photocopier was introduced. Imagine the learning curve with mimeograph machines and copy machines—the ink, the jams, the necessary precision of the paper placement in the tray. In the 1990s, the world "was introduced to the world wide web, connecting us to places and people in ways never seen before" (Huls, 2023). There have and will always be changes that we as educators encounter, and like always, we will find ways to adapt. No matter how many help tickets we send to our school's technology department or how long it takes us to figure it out, we will be okay, and so will our students.

As educators, we have seen the onset of many new advancements, in technology and otherwise; many trends come and go, and classrooms evolve each day and year. We are consistently challenged by how to navigate new texts, tools, and practices. AI is no different, and just as we found ways to become experts using the Smartboard, leveraging the onset of Google in our classrooms, and so forth, we will also find meaningful ways to use AI in our own learning and that of our students.

As we face challenges in education regarding text choices, equity, teacher shortages, and so much more, we hope that you can find ways to use AI in a manner that ushers in some excitement, creativity, and new discoveries. Research has shown time and time again that an effective educator can increase students' academic gains, reduce absenteeism, and improve a child's character development. The power of a good educator will always be what leaves a lasting impact on the life of a student (Chetty et al., 2014; Rockoff, 2004). During moments of uncertainty, we hope that you remember that your efforts matter greatly and have long-term effects on the students you show up for every day.

Using AI can help better prepare students to function in a world steeped in technology, while also supporting the important work educators embark upon each day. Navigating with care and thoughtful analysis, good educators can help the field of education, as well as individual classrooms, unlock the potentials of AI. Ultimately, the most important aspect of education involves the humans who are the center of it—students, educators, and families. No matter what changes and new aspects of learning may emerge, the heart of education will always be tethered to the people who make navigating the challenges so worthwhile.

There are many uncertainties about tomorrow, but at the heart of our classrooms, we know that two constants remain—our commitment to students, and the students themselves—and these two factors are what keep us grounded. It is because of this that we will keep learning, experimenting, trying, and evolving our practice. The hope of the future lies in the possibilities our students possess, and that is something that makes the unknowns and the fear of change ultimately worth it.

As we navigate the evolving landscape of AI in education and beyond, it's essential to remember that while technology can support, challenge, and even surprise us, it can never replace the deeply personal, lived experience of being human. Our greatest work as educators, creators, and community members is to remain connected to ourselves and one another in ways that no algorithm can replicate. We leave you with these words, as a reminder of what endures:

> What it is like to be us, in our full humanity—this isn't out there in the interwebs. It isn't stored in any archive, and the neural networks cannot be inward with what it feels like to be you, right now, looking at these words, looking away from these words to think about your life and our lives, turning from all this to your day and to what you will do in it, with others or alone. That can only *be lived*.
> (Burnett, 2025, p. 19)

References

Burnett, D. G. (2025, April 26). Will the humanities survive artificial intelligence? The New Yorker. https://www.newyorker.com/culture/the-weekend-essay/will-the-humanities-survive-artificial-intelligence

Chetty, R., Friedman, J. N., & Rockoff, J. E. (2014). Measuring the impacts of teachers I: Evaluating bias in teacher value-added estimates. *American Economic Review*, *104*(9), 2593–2632. https://doi.org/10.1257/aer.104.9.2593

Huls, A. (2023, July 10). The evolution of technology in K–12 classrooms: 1659 to today. *Technology Solutions That Drive Education*. https://edtechmagazine.com/k12/article/2022/01/evolution-technology-k-12-classrooms-1659-today-perfcon

Price, M. (2024, April 4). Council post: How AI and humans will transform the current education system. *Forbes*. www.forbes.com/sites/forbestechcouncil/2024/04/03/how-ai-and-humans-will-transform-the-current-education-system/

Rockoff, J. E. (2004). The impact of individual teachers on student achievement: Evidence from panel data. *American Economic Review*, *94*(2), 247–252. https://doi.org/10.1257/0002828041302244

Poetic Reflection

Gray Replaces White

Jordan Stempleman

When that last tree is in doubt
the love cannot scatter into recline

it's the time of tuna fish conditions
a kidney accident waiting to happen

a papaya cart that won't stop shaking
until turned over for good

and it's always the next phase that wants to know
if this time's for real
if this time's for good

to cheat while talking become quieter and easier
even quieter still

listen to the fangs tap downward against this mirror
as if to say
you are the beginning of some emptiness

always on my mind

Appendices

*Marlee S. Bunch and
Brittany R. Collins*

A defining principle of our collaborative work has always been a deep commitment to emphasizing and placing importance on both individual and collective reflection. We believe that self-assessment and moments of pause are foundational to doing the work discussed in previous chapters. Following are journal prompts and reflection questions regarding AI, culturally responsive teaching, and social-emotional learning, and the uses of AI in ELA (English language arts) and history/social studies content. We invite you to use these links and/or journal prompts to build on your learning. After the journal prompts, you will also find considerations to keep in mind when implementing AI in the classroom, tools to try out, and finally, additional resources and activities that offer actionable ways to begin using AI within student activities. By intentionally implementing AI, we can empower students to use technology responsibly, build classrooms that harness AI's potential, and preserve the human connection that makes our classrooms truly meaningful (Figure AP.1).

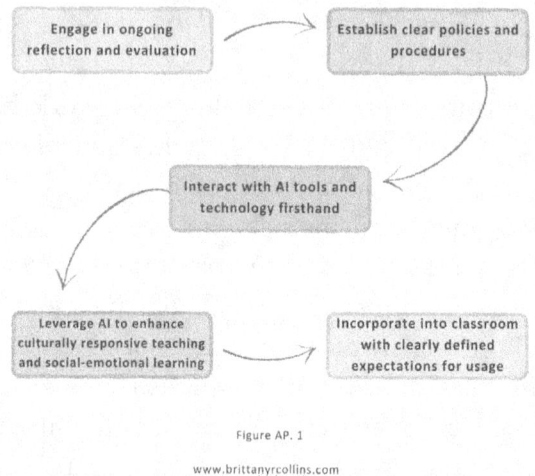

FIGURE AP.1 Intentional AI Usage Chart

Reflection and Journal Prompts:

AI and You

1. What are your greatest concerns about AI in the classroom? Can research help to clarify or alleviate any of your concerns? Where can you find more information to better understand your concerns?
2. What are your school or district policies (if any) regarding AI? Do you agree with these policies? Why or why not?
3. What are your classroom boundaries for using and incorporating AI? How might you involve students in the creation (and, as needed, revision) of these boundaries?
4. What leaders in your school, district, or extended professional community will support you in your learning journey regarding AI?

5. What excites you about AI? Where do you see potential and promise? How might you use AI to complement your lessons and classroom activities?
6. What are your non-negotiables regarding AI? How will you make these non-negotiables clear to students? How can you partner with students and families to craft what these parameters look like? Where will you post or share this information so that everyone has access to it?
7. Make a list of the biases, misinformation, or inequitable information that might concern you about AI. Then, create a plan for how you will create supplemental information to counter what AI produces and build cultural competence among students and fellow coworkers.
8. What support or resources do you need to successfully and intentionally integrate AI into your classroom? How might you engage your school or local community in garnering these supports and resources?
9. When AI evolves and changes, what do you imagine you might need to do in order to keep your lessons, activities, and classroom procedures current and relevant?
10. Reflect on what fears or concerns you might have about the vast and ever-changing aspects of education (including technology). What aspects of education and learning do you want to maintain and keep intact? What might need revision or updates? How can AI help connect students to society, global learning, etc.?

AI and Your Students

1. How will you know that students have a clear understanding of the benefits and limitations of AI? What points will you discuss with students when you begin introducing AI in your classroom?

2. What are the consequences if students misuse AI? How will you enforce this accountability? How will you ensure consequences fall within restorative justice framing?
3. How will you explain to students that AI carries bias and racial discrimination, and is connected to systemic inequities? How can you use this moment to begin building a culturally responsive space, leveraging the foundation of this discussion?
4. What will you say in your syllabus and/or classroom agreement about the use of AI?
5. How can students use AI to tap into their creativity? Ask students for input and examples.
6. Discuss a recent article or story about AI. What do you notice are the pros/cons, and how can we use the information from the article you found in our classroom?
7. If you had to choose one subject that you are likely to use AI the most for, what would it be and why?
8. What are some of the ways you have explored or used AI? Which ones do you find most useful and why?
9. In what ways can students help lead discussions and activities where AI is utilized, and how might this benefit building a classroom that uses AI in a responsible and intentional manner?

AI and Culturally Responsive Teaching

1. When creating lessons or activities, how do you consider the ways that AI can support culturally responsive teaching? What tools do you use?
2. How do you already incorporate culturally responsive teaching in your classroom? What are two or three successful lessons or activities that you could add an AI learning component to?
3. Consider creating 1–2 lessons that center culturally responsive teaching. How will you use AI in these lessons

to build interactions, communication, discussion, etc.? Think about possible group projects or interactive activities (e.g., jigsaw, Socratic seminar).
4. What are two AI tools that could support English language learners? How do you plan to incorporate these tools?
5. What are two AI tools that could help you teach students about other cultures, communities? What could these same tools teach students about global learning?
6. AI has many tools that help with storytelling—can you identify one or two you would be willing to try? What stories do you think need to be elevated and unearthed? What stories do you think have been overlooked?

AI and Social-Emotional Learning

1. How can AI help support your learning goals for social-emotional learning?
2. Locate one AI tool that supports social-emotional learning. How can you incorporate this tool into your classroom?
3. Find one credible source that offers you information about the social and emotional development and competencies of youth at the grade level you teach. Next, find one AI tool that would help you incorporate this information into your pedagogy or classroom.
4. Two aspects of social-emotional learning are safety and the importance of meaningful, respectful relationships. How do you believe AI tools can support safety in the classroom? How do you believe AI can support relationship-building? What perils should educators and students be aware of regarding AI in connection with safety and relationships?
5. Find one AI tool that offers a mindfulness activity you would be willing to use with students. What are the

benefits of the activity or tool? What are the shortfalls? How might you use it in conjunction with a lesson or unit?
6. Pick one of the five core social-emotional competencies (as defined by CASEL, 2023)—self-awareness, social awareness, self-management, relationship skills, and responsible decision-making—that you most hope to prioritize in your classroom.
7. Consider a tension or conflict that you are encountering in your practice. Use an AI tool to either generate some scripts that might help you navigate this scenario or to simulate a conversation related to the scenario. What resonates from this interaction? What takeaways might you apply to the real-life dynamic?
8. Among one group of learners, you may witness a variety of social-emotional strengths and areas for growth. Using an AI tool, create a plan to differentiate your SEL instruction, tailoring content to the skills and competencies each student, or group of students, is most focused on.
9. Return to Chapter 3, Applying AI to Human-Centered Pedagogy and survey the various AI use cases related to executive functioning (EF). What are your students' greatest EF needs? How are you currently working to meet them, and how might AI tools help you to further scaffold or differentiate this approach?
10. How might you use AI text generators to create stories, activities, scripts, or scenarios that engage students in conversation about social-emotional skills relevant to their developmental stage and, optionally, the subject area that you teach (Collins, 2021)?

AI and English Language Arts (ELA)

1. Ask students to help you brainstorm a list of prompts to ask AI about literary elements and devices. This can be a good way to introduce a novel, theme, or character of a

text. Having prewritten prompts helps to keep students focused and ensures that the responses they get from AI are useful.
2. Choose one aspect of writing that you would like to help students work on. Consider how AI can help students improve their writing and the revision process.
3. How can you use AI to help students with tone in writing? Mechanics? Clarity? Readability?
4. In what ways can you use AI to supplement texts in the classroom? How might you use AI tools to offer additional literary benefits to students? How might you use AI tools to offer additional perspectives about the primary text(s) and supplemental text(s)?
5. Instead of students using ChatGPT to cheat, how can they use it as a companion to their own writing journey? Ask the class to generate a list of ways that ChatGPT can assist or enhance their writing. If you were to begin that list, what would you put at the top?
6. When and how might you incorporate Jordan Stempleman's poems, and the AI-related activities related to them, into your existing ELA units?
7. How can you connect modern discourses regarding AI to themes of tradition vs. modernity, humans vs. nature vs. technology, regression vs. innovation, etc., represented in the literature you teach?
8. What peer review or workshop activities do you currently incorporate in ELA? How can you add AI as a third perspective in these existing procedures, using the activities in this text?
9. To facilitate the "AI Educators" activity, in which students practice informational writing skills and teach younger students about ethical AI use, what connections might you forge in your school or local community? (Tight on time? An AI tool can help you generate outreach emails.)

AI and History and/or Social Studies

1. In what ways might AI be able to support inclusive histories in your classroom? Can you name specific examples of what this could look like?
2. Give students an AI-generated essay, grade it with a rubric as a class, and then ask students to work in groups to make it more culturally responsive. Students can use the principles of the un/HUSH framework mentioned in previous pages and referenced in Figure 2.3 to guide them in activity. After the activity, ask students the following questions: What did you notice about the AI essay? What was needed to make it more culturally responsive? Did using the framework as a guide help to improve the essay (why or why not)? You can journal in response to these questions, too.
3. What histories are connected to your students? How can AI illuminate these histories? What tools could help you bring these histories into the classroom? How can AI help you add context and truth to these histories?
4. How can AI help you bring primary sources into the classroom? Identify two interesting primary sources that might spark your next lesson.
5. How might you use AI tools to incorporate images that teach about historical time periods, movements, people, etc.? Share the image with the class, asking students to analyze the image and generate questions they have.
6. Experiment with the AI tool Hello History: www.hellohistory.ai/. Choose one historical figure to begin a conversation with. Reflect on the pros/cons of the tool. Would students be engaged? How could you pair the tool with a lesson? How could you make the activity academically worthwhile? What context might students need to get more out of the historical discussions they encounter, and how can you front-load this information?

7. How might you use AI tools to make your history lessons more accessible to your students, whether through content generated in multiple Lexile levels, the creation of multimodal content, etc.?
8. Might there be a role for AI-generated historical fiction in your curricula? For example, might your students prompt AI to create historical fiction stories about the period or context you are studying, then analyze their accuracy and cultural responsiveness? Consider how AI can infuse creativity and critical thinking into your current plans.
9. Test several AI tools that allow for simulated interaction with historical figures, such as character.ai or D-ID (www.d-id.com/). The latter allows you to create videos and avatars of historical figures, for example. What role might these tools play in bringing history to life for your students? How can you spark critical thinking and discussion about historical accuracy and cultural responsiveness using these tools?
10. What is your favorite "hidden history" to teach, and why? How might AI tools support you in teaching this lesson that you love?

A good tool to continuously assess AI and its usage in your classroom is your own understanding of how you will allow AI to be used in your classroom. Again, self-reflection and experimentation are key. As mentioned in previous chapters, having a clear understanding of your personal views, classroom usage, and various AI tools is a good place to start. Once you establish some foundational procedures, boundaries, and expectations, you will want to decide whether or not students can use AI in assignments. In the following pages, you will find an AI policy template to help you create your own, along with a tool to help determine when AI will be permitted for use with assignments. Perhaps some assignments will have optional AI sections, others will ask that students experiment with an AI tool, and still others might ask that students not use AI at all. We encourage you to find ways to allow for varied options, as this gives students the chance to see that the tools we have to learn with may evolve, but foundational aspects of learning, such as curiosity, mentorship, research, and inquiry, remain constant.

Consider the examples in Figures AP.2 and AP.3 for guidance on setting up a similar approach in your classroom to demonstrate how AI will be integrated and utilized. Whatever expectations and guardrails you and your students decide upon, everything should be put in writing, discussed with students, and shared with families. Learning tools that have clear expectations coupled with regular reflection and discussion help to maintain human-centered learning and growth. Understanding your own stance regarding AI will offer students clear parameters and clarity regarding boundaries and expectations, which will result in better outcomes for everyone.

In addition to creating an AI policy, consider establishing clear expectations for using AI with assignments. The chart in Figure AP.3, inspired by M. Forbes and J. Brandauer in the article "What's My Stance on GenAI in This Class?" from the Gettysburg College Johnson Center for Teaching and Learning, will help you assess whether or not AI should be permitted for various assignments and activities. You can re-create this chart for your learning space or use it as a guide when planning lessons.

AI Tools to Be Familiar With and Try Out

Experimenting with AI tools is important as you and your students work to discover emerging best practices for using AI in the classroom (Mollick, 2024). While not an exhaustive list, the following tools encompass LLMs (large language models) such as ChatGPT, Microsoft Copilot in Bing; image generators such as Adobe Firefly; and sound generators such as Soundraw (OpenAI, 2024).

Classroom AI Policies & Procedures

Use this policy (Figure AP.2) document to outline your classroom's commitment to intentional and equity-minded usage of technology and AI tools.

I. Introduction

Provide a brief overview of the document and the importance of intentional use and assessment of AI tools in your classroom. Explain the relationship between your classroom's values and AI so that you can show that AI is a tool that will be used to compliment learning.

II. Definitions and Concepts

Define key terms related to AI and provide context for their use. It is optional to include culturally relevant learning and social-emotional learning definitions, though it would help reiterate your intent to use AI in a manner that benefits all students and avoids the concerns of AI bias and misinformation.

AI Tools	Share a definition of any AI terms you want to clarify and a list of some AI tools you find valuable. Mention how you will help ensure that AI benefits your classroom.
Culturally Relevant Learning	Share a definition of the term and why it matters to your classroom and building a culture of acceptance and equitable practices (this is an optional section).
Social Emotional Learning	Share a definition of the term and why it matters to your classroom and student learning (this is an optional section).

III. Responsibilities and Accountabilities

Identify how the class will work collectively to implement and maintaining the responsible use of AI. Include your students in this process for clarity and buy-in.

IV. Trying Out the Tech, Assessment and Education

Describe the ways in which you will prepare your classroom and students for using AI. What tools will you try out? How will AI be implemented and assessed? How will you teach students about the benefits and perils of AI, so that it is used in effective and equitable ways?

Resource	Frequency	Description
Plan for Introducing Class to AI	Start of school year with periodic updates	Write a descriptive overview of the plan for introducing your students, families, and classroom to AI.
Social Emotional Learning Procedures, and Expectations	Quarterly	Write a descriptive overview of the policies, resource and procedures you will discuss and provide for students and families.
Try Out the Tech Practice and Assessment	Weekly	Write a descriptive overview of the resources, or opportunities you will provide for students to try AI tools and assess these tools use, equity, outcomes, and so forth.

V. Statement of Commitment

State your classroom's commitment to the ethical, collaborative, innovative, and culturally responsive use of AI and the goals you aim to achieve. Describe the process for evaluating and improving the use of AI and its implementation.

VI. Stakeholders

Identify the key stakeholders and individuals involved in the implementation and maintenance of AI in your school/district/classroom. In other words, who will students or families contact if they have questions or concerns? You may want to consider appointing a student as an AI sponsor or classroom representative.

Title	Name	Responsibilities
You (Teacher)	Insert name	Add details of this person's role.
School Administrator or Technology Admin	Insert name	Add details of this person's role.
Student Sponsor	Insert name	Add details of this person's role.
Parent/Family Representative	Insert name	Add details of this person's role.

VII. Conclusion

Summarize the key points of the document and reaffirm your commitment to using technology and AI ethically and responsibly. Add any closing thoughts that are important to mention.

FIGURE AP.2 Example of an AI Classroom Policy

AI Free Zone (No)	AI Open Zone (Yes)	Conditional Zone (Maybe)
Assignment is high stakes and requires analysis and thinking that does not rely on AI.	Schedule regular check-ins with students to discuss how they are using AI and what benefits and/or struggles they are experiencing. Design a feedback tool or survey to accompany these check-in meetings.	Model for students how you would like them to ideally use specific AI tools. Walk through these tools together as a class and assess which ones work best for certain assignments and activities.
Create a rubric that overviews the objectives of the assignment and how it will be graded, so students know why AI is off limits.	Use free AI tools and ensure that you cite sources for which tools you used during the assignment.	Create a warm-up or practice exercise so students can familiarize themselves with AI tools you might suggest they utilize for the assignment. Provide a list of these preferred AI tools and where to access them.
The assignment should ask a prompt or question that relies on deep thinking and critical thinking.	Use AI to help develop a culturally responsive assessment or metric for how AI will be incorporated into the assignment/activity/project. Clear objectives matter.	Offer students very specific information regarding how AI can and should be used in the assignment. Give a rationale with examples regarding why.
The assignment should be relevant and current.	Offer a space for students to debrief and discuss their experiences using AI with the assignment or project. Remember to maintain the human-centered aspects of learning.	Offer a space for students to debrief and discuss their experiences using AI with the assignment or project. Offer opportunities for reflection.

FIGURE AP.3 Can Students Use AI With Assignments?

Most AI tools have free versions you can use, though keep in mind that the free and paid versions can slightly differ. Each previous chapter offered a section called "Try Out the Tech," where we encouraged you to explore certain tools. We are again encouraging and inviting you to spend time trying out various offerings, as this is one of the best ways to understand the benefits and limitations of each and how they might complement or enhance aspects of learning in your classroom. The sources listed below (AP.1 AI Tools to Try) are just a small starting point; we invite you to keep and expand a running list of your own, tailored to your unique teaching and learning needs and objectives.

> **Box AP.1 AI Tools to Try**

Adobe Firefly: Generates images and text effects
Audio Open: Transforms voice notes (articles, memos, emails, etc.) into publish-ready text

Bing: Uses a large language model to search the Internet similar to a search engine

ChatGPT: Responds to text prompts and generates text through a conversational interface

Claude: Uses language processing to create a conversational interface

Curipod: Generates a slide deck that can include interactive aspects such as polls, word clouds, open-ended questions, etc.

Dall-E: Generates computer graphics from text prompts

Khanmigo: Tutors students through a Socratic chatbot

MagicSchool: Creates lesson plans, classroom activities, assessments, and more

Pictory: Transforms written lessons or articles into video content using AI

Stable Diffusion AI: Transforms text to images

Soundraw: Generates royalty-free music

Please note that this is not an exhaustive list.

AI Warm-Ups

The following QR code links to resources and warm-up activities (quick exercises designed to explore AI) across various subject areas, created by the AI Education Project (aiEDU, 2025). These activities can also be used for short group work and provide a user-friendly way to begin integrating AI into daily classroom routines.

Additional Resources to Consider

For those eager to learn more about artificial intelligence, whether from a technical perspective or in continued connection with education, we invite you to explore the following additional resources—which, like the previously mentioned tools, are merely a starting place (Vento, 2023).

Books and News Outlets

AI Literacy Fundamentals by Ben Jones
Artificial Negligence by James Wilson
Artificial Intelligence: A Guide for Thinking Humans by Melanie Mitchell
Co-Intelligence: Living and Working With AI by Dr. Ethan Mollick
The Encyclopedia of Educational Equity by Dr. Shannon Anderson
The Alignment Problem by Brian Christian
Unmasking AI by Dr. Joy Buolamwini
Edutopia—This site offers many articles written by practicing teachers related to AI in the classroom; filter by the relevant tag to read AI-related content.
Education Week—An education news outlet that runs content written by practitioners regarding AI innovations as related to education.
The Bean Path—A resource hub that offers tools and information regarding AI.
The 74—An education news outlet with pieces penned by students, teachers, and school leaders regarding AI.

Podcasts

The following podcasts can be found on Apple or Spotify:

AI Breakdown
AI Today Podcast
Eye on AI
Practical AI

Social Justice in Technology

The following organizations work to create equity and justice related to AI and offer information and resources:

>Civics of Technology
>AI Now Institute
>AI for the People
>Algorithmic Justice League
>Berkman Klein Center for Internet Studies at Harvard University
>Center for Information Technology Policy at Princeton University
>Center for Media Justice
>Cobb Payton
>ColorCoded
>Data & Society Research Institute
>Design Justice
>Equitable Internet Initiative
>#MoreThanCode
>UCLA Center for Critical Internet Inquiry

We hope that these additional tools offer opportunities to explore, examine, and experiment.

References

aiEDU. (2025). *AI toolkits.* https://www.aiedu.org/
CASEL. (2023, March 3). What is the CASEL framework? https://casel.org/fundamentals-of-sel/what-is-the-casel-framework/
Collins, B. (2021). *Learning from loss: A trauma-informed approach to supporting grieving students.* Heinemann.
Forbes, M., & Brandauer, J. (n.d.). What's my stance on genAI in this class? *Gettysburg College Johnson Center for Teaching and Learning.* https://genai.sites.gettysburg.edu/positions-and-policies/

Mollick, E. (2024). Co-intelligence: Living and working with AI. *Portfolio/Penguin*.

OpenAI. (2024). *ChatGPT* (January 8 version) [Large language model]. https://chat.openai.com/chat

Vento, C. (2023, November 15). Top AI tools for ELA teachers. *ReadTheory*. https://readtheory.org/teachers-lounge/top-ai-tools-for-ela-teachers/

Afterword

Cameron Alleyne

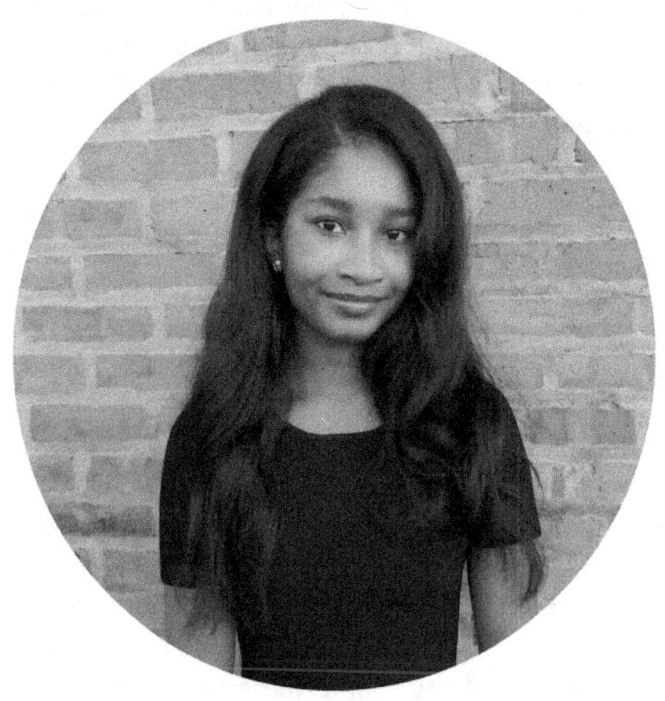

Cameron Alleyne is an aspiring writer/journalist from Queens, New York. She will be starting college in the Fall of 2025 and plans to major in English. She has written blogs for Write the World, a nonprofit that provides teens with an online writing space. She has also attended NYU's Urban Journalism Program and the Kenyon Review Young Writers Workshop. Outside of writing, she enjoys learning about history, baking, watching reality TV, reading, doodling in her notebook, traveling, and sipping a hot latte. Connect with her on LinkedIn at: www.linkedin.com/in/cameron-a-178594285/

The year is 2074. Over the remnants of what once was a traditional classroom, a computer is lurking. The students are slumped over in their seats as they read generated sentence after generated sentence. On the outskirts of society, educators, creatives, and their allies are locked in fiercely guarded cells. The children of tomorrow cannot read or write proficiently under the techno-overlord's control. Borrowing from input data spanning many, many years, AI covers more ground than a person ever could. The end of the world is upon us!

Or not.

On October 10, 2024, Elon Musk revealed the Optimus robots, AI-powered Optimus humanoid robots, which are supposed to make consumers' lives easier. Musk claimed they could do just about anything, including teaching or babysitting, making them the technology of the future. Watching them perform human tasks with their sleek design and robotic movements felt like something straight out of a dystopian sci-fi film. Although the *Los Angeles Times* went on to report that the robots were somewhat operated by people throughout the event, discourse regarding the robots had been sparked. Social media platforms lit up with a storm of reactions ranging from eager to disillusioned with the direction of technology. The thought of AI coming into human form seems frightening. But, for many people, these conversations were held long before the unveiling of Musk's newest invention.

Doomsday scenario aside, art, writing, and education have all been the focus of discourse regarding generative AI. We have reached an awkward state where many people appreciate art but deprecate artists. Being told that AI can do exactly what we can do, only without the inspiration, creative process, or time spent isn't encouraging. As a high school student, I've been left with one foot in and one foot out when it comes to pursuing my passion. I have always loved writing and journalism, but it seems like everyone thinks that field will vanish.

Do you know the response people give you when you tell them you're majoring in English? That "Oh . . . but maybe it would be wise to double major." ChatGPT only exacerbated the struggle. Before, the subtext of "Oh . . . an English major?" was "I don't know what kind of job you get with that, and I don't think you'll make a lot of money," which: A. ouch, and B. maybe kind of true but still a little misguided. The humanities are applicable and important. Writers, journalists, historians, anthropologists, and artists all contribute to everyday life.

Now, I've also been told, "Oh, well, you know about ChatGPT and all of that stuff . . ." I tell them that I do know, and I am not worried, but sometimes, I can't help but wonder if I am just delusional.

The first time I remember seeing AI art was of an image of a kitten on X. Its uncanny features and atypical proportions made it easily identifiable to me, but I came to realize that wasn't the case for others. Since that time, I've seen dozens of videos and images that were clearly AI to me but not to other viewers, especially those who were older. The same applies to writing. What is overly robotic to one person could be perfectly acceptable to another. Although we would probably like to think that we could never be fooled, think about when we get older and technology improves. With this discrepancy, the power of AI becomes daunting. Now, people have an incentive to use AI to mislead others through hyper-realistic text or images on social media. As AI art becomes more normalized, companies can cut corners by using AI to do what a person would have done before. People can create whatever they want even if it can bring harm to others. In a school environment, this can translate into cyberbullying and harassment. With time, we can expect school administrators across the country to be ready to respond, but as headline after headline comes out about students using AI in negative ways, it seems like we all have a long way to go.

With all the reasons to use AI, why even bother to create? Quite simply, I think that AI can be that good but not "stage-a-complete-takeover" good.

I've been in classes where students who used AI throughout the entire school year got decent grades, but they didn't outperform me or other students who actually did the work. Even though some students haven't been swayed by the introduction of ChatGPT, that doesn't mean its presence isn't felt by all students. For everyone I know who has never used AI for school, there is someone who has, whether it was a one-time thing or habitually. Nevertheless, at times, the differences in our academic performances aren't drastic; that fosters some feelings of bitterness. However, when AI is approached in a way that is more constructive, students may feel less inclined to use it unethically.

I imagine the anxiety teachers feel is different because whether you're working for or against AI is heavily influenced by others. I've had teachers express a lot of frustration with AI-generated classwork and homework. Some of my teachers have put more emphasis on in-class work. Others have continuously gone through the process of detecting and reporting AI work. Whether you're fighting to eradicate all workarounds for students to complete their work with AI or you're trying to find a healthy balance, there isn't a clear blueprint to follow. That doesn't mean that all teachers are incredibly fearful or frustrated with AI as a whole. From my high school teachers, I've heard varying stances on its place in school and beyond. One of my teachers shared that he felt somewhat indifferent about AI being used in commercials because he feels that AI art and traditional art can coexist in some places. I had another teacher say that it wasn't something that worried him because he felt that our assignments were so tedious that AI could "only take us so far" anyway. I even have a teacher who consults AI to gauge what an inauthentic student response may look like. That doesn't mean that teachers taking the reins on AI use are ineffective, though. So far, I have only had two teachers who had an AI policy outside of a firm ban on use: my art teacher and my research teacher. For my art class, we can use AI for reference images. For my research class, we have one massive research project spanning over the course of the entire school year, complete with a report and presentation. In that class, we can use AI to guide our research process. In both of these classes, things operate smoothly. After being told that we could use AI in art class, our pens, paintbrushes, and creative drive didn't disintegrate on the spot. While the option is available, my classmates and I have found our own ways to satisfy the class requirements with or without AI. Similarly, in my research class, the work we do is so thorough and tedious that the involvement of AI could only take us so far. Although I don't doubt that AI serves as a temptation for some of my classmates, I don't think it is a crutch. I haven't used AI for any of my classes, but I'm not opposed to using it in a way that the teachers have allowed us to. Using AI as an assisting tool is different from using it as a way to escape work.

AI can also have an influence on students' long-term choices. A good friend of mine, who is an incredibly talented artist, expressed to me that she would no longer be studying animation because she felt like the industry wasn't truly secure. I had another friend tell me that she expected journalism to fade out of existence, too. Hearing students around me associate their passions with inevitable obscurity is demoralizing. Our future should be a horizon begging to be explored, not a slowly decaying path. There will always be a place for human-made work in our world.

Let us return to the sci-fi dystopian world. Picture this: mass destruction, evil scientists, even more evil robots, all the usual stuff. But, keep in mind that spirit, passion, and creativity can coexist with changing technology. Also keep in mind that not all scientists are actually evil, and there are people out there, including students, who are just as willing to reshape AI use as you are. So even in the event of a techno-apocalypse, not everything is lost.

Of course, the future is scary, but fear is paralyzing, so ruminating only stagnates progress.

What makes teachers so important is their adaptability. Through pandemics, new approaches, and a changing political landscape that warp classroom teaching (past and present), teachers have stuck it out. The teachers I have gotten to know at this stage in my life, as a high school senior, have shaped me in a multitude of ways. They've shown me the role of empathy, hard work, stick-to-itiveness, irony, disillusionment, and honesty in learning inside and outside of the classroom.

I or anyone else can't surely determine what direction academia will go in with regard to AI, but I do know that as long as teachers such as Ms. Collins and Dr. Bunch, among many others, are as focused and passionate as before, students are in good hands. At least as long as evil robots don't attack.

We invite you to read and discover more from Dr. Marlee S. Bunch and Brittany R. Collins:

- *THE MAGNITUDE OF US* (BUNCH, 2024) TCPRESS.COM
- *UNLEARNING THE HUSH* (BUNCH, 2025) PRESS.UILLINOIS.EDU
- *LEARNING FROM LOSS* (COLLINS, 2021) HEINEMANN.COM
- *HOW WE BEAR IT: WOMEN WITH INVISIBLE ILLNESSES* (COLLINS, FORTHCOMING)

For Product Safety Concerns and Information please contact our EU
representative GPSR@taylorandfrancis.com
Taylor & Francis Verlag GmbH, Kaufingerstraße 24, 80331 München, Germany

www.ingramcontent.com/pod-product-compliance
Lightning Source LLC
Chambersburg PA
CBHW061828300426

44115CB00013B/2292